Bruno Marion

Chaos, A User's Guide

**Solutions for developing ourselves, our
communities and organizations in a chaotic world**

*May the future
be with you !*

B. M

For Kai

Content

Introduction 1

User manual.. 5

Part One 7

    Number.. 10
    Speed 11
    Inter-connectivity 13
    The chaos of information 18
    Has the world gone mad? 20
    The energy crisis 21
    Financial crisis 23
    Social crisis 25
    Ecological crisis 28

Part Two 31

    Acquiring the right lenses 33
    First revolution: how long does it take to fill your
    bathtub?.. 36
    Second revolution: all is relative!.......................... 38
    Third revolution: a quantum leap 39
    Why the chaos theories are important for you?.... 40

The importance of the theory of chaos 42
Fourth revolution: the theories of chaos 44
The evolution of chaotic systems 46
What is a Fractal? 54

Part Three 67

Giving up the linear binary vision 69
From linear/binary vision to fractal vision: when the
great Asian and Western philosophies meet 72
East / West, a more fractal way of interpreting 73
Duality / Non-duality 73
Permanence / Impermanence 75
Linear or cyclic time 76
The teleological / morphological world 77
Truth or the path 78
Truth, good and beauty 80
Our species is evolving – and you? (Beauty) 82
Kevin's life: how life has become fractal 82
Fractal identities: Who am I? 86
The search for the authentic being 90
Your brain is fractal and chaotic! 92
The fractal being 97
Organizing one's life fractally? 98
    Work-time / leisure-time: 98
    Work-space / personal life-space: 99
    Home-space / holiday-space: 99
    Learning time / work time / retirement time: .. 100
    Salary time / job-hunting time: 101
    Working life / time for religion-spirituality: ... 101
More fractal bio-rhythms: sources of depression,
illness or evolution? 103
How to take right decisions in a chaotic world? 108
Going further: Fractal consciousness? Fractal
universe? 110
The evolution of our cultures and our social
relationships (Goodness) 114

A 'fractal' love-relationship? 114
A new world culture? 118
A fractal world culture 119
The world according to Huntington... and the world
we want to build! 123
The evolution of writing 125
Analytic writing 126
Analog writing (Chinese) 128
A more fractal civilization and humanity 131
A new fractal ethic 135
The emergence of a new collective fractal
consciousness: it is already there! 138
Beyond the real 142
Living together, the analogy with life 144
The Collective: a more fractal society, institutions,
learning and organizations? (The true) 147
Towards a more just, more efficient, more fractal
democracy? 147
A digression: are polls/surveys to be believed? . 151
A more fractal production-consumption-elimination
chain? 154
Fractal energy networks 158
A fractal galaxy of currencies 161
Education 163
Conceptual Western education or practical Eastern
learning: towards a fractal integration? 164
A less linear allocation of spaces and of learning
ages 166
Understanding and developing our
organizations 170
The fractal organization 170
Organizations in fractal hives 174
Self-organization: how to maintain the survival of a
team, an organization, a company, in a chaotic
system? 177
Regulatory processes in organizations 182

Sport as a process of regulation.......................... 187
Diversity in a fractal organization 188
What vision for a fractal company or
organization?.. 189
The systems of information in a fractal
organization.. 190
The fractal manager.. 192
Time management and priorities in a turbulent and
chaotic world.. 196
Fractal methodology for resolving problems 199

Conclusion... 205

A bright future: emergence is possible............... 207
Long live the butterflies! 209

Bibliography 213

Introduction

Chaos is my friend

Bob Dylan

When people ask me what I do, I usually tell them: "I spend half my time trying to understand the world and the other half explaining it to others."

So, for 25 years (much longer according to my parents) I have been trying to understand the world around me. After the usual school-boy experiments, growing bean-seeds and the like, I figured I could understand the world by becoming an engineer. I did learn a few things – but not enough to really figure out the world. I realized that it was no longer science that governed the world but economics and business – it was no longer a world of engineers but of storekeepers, financiers and company lawyers. And so, I decided to get an MBA. But that again did not take me any closer to finding answers to my fundamental questions of the world.

It dawned on me then that the answer was not in my part of the world but maybe ... on the other side. I thought I needed to look at things from the other side of the planet

1

and I was off on a world-tour looking for other cultures, especially the Eastern. I travelled for a whole year, at a time when neither internet nor mobiles existed. I had only a backpack that contained my shorts, t-shirts, and below them a suit, two shirts and a pair of city shoes. Those travels were about the encounter of the West and the East and led to my first book, *Asia, Business and Good Manners,* which was the first business guide for Asia. This book was followed by others. The last to be published was *Succeeding with the Asians*.

Well, my search continued.

I thought I should return, after all, to the base: philosophy. So, like an enthusiastic novice discovering the main approaches in philosophy, I began studying both the Western and Eastern schools, from ancient times leading up to the Integral philosophy which, without any doubt, is the approach most in resonance with my own vision and our present-day world.

Since, with an around the world trip almost every year and several years of meditation, at last I have the answer; at this moment I know I will never find the answer to "how the world works, but I have discovered that the path leading to the answer is itself a part of the answer.

I have also observed that the sciences, philosophies, spiritual disciplines, the East, the West, all converge very harmoniously, and this convergence can give us new keys for understanding this changing world.

I wish to share with you what I have discovered and learned along the way. I want to show you that the world is getting better and better, it is getting worse and worse, faster and faster, to the point where the world has become turbulent and chaotic.

I will also give you some very simple tools that are based on one of the most advanced domains of science: the theories of chaos. And these tools will help you to analyze, understand and thus act in the turbulent, chaotic world that we live in.

And finally, I will share with you some practical, concrete examples. We shall then see how we can use new lenses and new tools in order to live and act in this fast-changing world. We shall see how to understand and live our personal and family lives, how to behave in our organizations, our associations, our companies – in this world overrun by an avalanche of changes.

CHAOS, A USER'S GUIDE

User manual

These days nobody reads user manuals… so I shall be brief.

I am not going to expound a theory in this book but rather a method. It does not follow a logical linear course where, in order to understand B, you need to understand A first and to understand C you first need to go through A and then B and so forth. We shall rather discover and build together a mosaic, a puzzle where each new piece could be added in any order. We will, in fact, discover that it is a sort of a fractal image! In the beginning it doesn't look like much but then, progressively, an image comes into focus. To the point where you cannot doubt the reality of such an image. And as we go further, this image becomes more clearly accurate. I invite you, then, to explore this new picture of the world that we shall construct and discover together!

In order to help you understand the origin of my approach and place it in context, I have included a bibliography at the end of the book that lists some of the books I have read that have helped me to construct the train of thought that guides this book.

This is not a book that explains what the future will be, but it is a guide that will make you capable of constructing the future you wish.

Part One

**The world is getting better and better
It is getting worse and worse
Faster and faster**

In this first part, I would like to 'take stock of the world' with you. I want to show how our world is getting better and better, worse and worse, faster and faster. I would like to show that it is not in equilibrium, nowhere close to it. The world has indeed become turbulent and chaotic.

This 'chaos', those turbulences, which we will see in the second part are a 'natural' evolution of mankind, lead to what is more commonly called crisis: social, economic and financial, cultural, ecological, personal crises, crises of meaning. We also return to these crises in the fourth part: how to protect themselves and also how to take advantage of them.

Why has the world become turbulent? Essentially for three reasons: number, speed and connectivity. We shall describe in this first part the great changes in humanity in terms of number, speed and inter-connectivity. We shall then see in the second part how the theories of chaos show us that these changes are the cause of this turbulence and chaos.

Number

How many of us were on earth 150 years ago? 1 billion. How many are we today? 7 billion. During the last years, within hardly a few generations, the population grew incredibly. We have gone from 2 to 7 billion in just one generation.

We could then say that while our parents lived in a world that was empty, we live in one that is full. A world that is full and that will get, as we shall see, more and more connected.

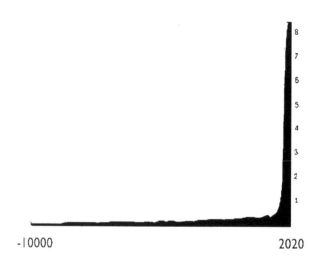

Human population curve

Speed

This is a world that is moving faster and faster.

The lithosphere (mineral) evolved over billions of years. The biosphere (life) evolved over millions of years. The noosphere (information) is now measured in nanoseconds!

At the scale of human history, it took man 3 million years to go from the 'hunter & gathering' era to 'agriculturist & breeding' era; then 30,000 years to enter the era of 'industry & commerce'; and only 300 years to pass into the age of 'creation & communication'. Technological, social and economic revolutions happen today over two generations or even a single one. Neither human beings nor cultures have time for gradual adaptation. For example, our grandparents came into the world, worked and died close to the same geographical place, but for us today this seems highly unlikely! Similarly, the 1000 words of common conversation that our parents learned were, with very few exceptions, the same 1000 words they would use at the end of their life. The 1000 words that you use most commonly now are already quite different from the ones you learned as a young person. Not that long ago you did not *download* or *twit* or *podcast*, nor did you send *texts messages* or receive *emails*.

The world of commerce and especially finance, a historical human activity, has also accelerated in an unbelievable way. Trades that took weeks or even months on foot or on horseback or by ship just a few hundred years ago, happen today, in the world of finance, in 'High Frequency Trading' or 'High Speed Trading'. Stock market orders take place in 150 millionth of a second. And this isn't an exceptional occurrence; nearly half the stock orders today for the shares at the Paris Stock Exchange are passed by two High Speed Trading companies, over two-thirds at the New York Stock Exchange.

Time is speeding up.

Inter-connectivity

On 4th August 1938, an exploratory expedition of the American Museum of Natural History looking for new species of birds in New Guinea, changed human history. Entering the Great Valley of the Balim River, which was thought to be uninhabited, Richard Archbold and his colleagues were surprised to find a culture with a population of over 50,000 people. They experienced what was to be the last 'first encounter'. For one of the last time in human history, men and women who were completely ignorant of each other's existence in a part of the planet met.

500 years ago, a human being had little chance of meeting over a 1000 people in his or her lifetime.

In 1900, 11 cities had over 1 million inhabitants. In 1950, there were 75. In 1976, their number rose to 191. Today 414 cities have more than 1 million inhabitants, of which 271 – more than 50 percent – are in China.

What percentage of the population lives today in the cities? Approximately 50 percent. Besides growing, the human population has concentrated in few places.

Today, as you are reading these lines, as every moment, 1 million people are flying above our heads. Over 50,000 flights land and take off each day in the world and make it possible for millions of people to meet.

People are crossing and meeting each other more and more.

They also communicate more and more.

One evening, I was returning from dinner at the home of a friend of mine who lives on a barge next to the Bir Hakeim Bridge in Paris. On the right bank of the Seine, we reached the Alma tunnel, but it was impossible to enter because it had been closed. At that moment we noticed a chase: a policeman was trying to tackle what seemed to be a journalist or, at any rate, someone loaded with cameras, against the floor. At the other end of the tunnel, we saw dozens of vehicles, police cars, fire-engines, ambulances with all lights turned on. Was it a gas-leak? A terrorist attack? No, just an accident in a Paris road tunnel.

For those of you who have not watched television for ten years, Princess Diana had died.

Moments later, 2.5 billion people in more than 190 countries, watched Princess Diana's funeral being telecast in 44 languages. This number constituted about 40 percent of the total population then. Even if the much lower estimates of 500 million were to be accepted, it was still the most watched event in the history of television! A car accident in Paris changed, at least for a while, the life of an important number of people around the world.

On 26th December in 2004, I was on the road between Chennai and Pondicherry in south India, when a journalist, unaware of the fact that I was in India, called me on my French mobile wanting to know my reaction to the 'event'. And this is how I came to know that I was in that very part of the country that had been most affected by the Tsunami. A total of 225,000 people had been killed and millions rendered homeless in Asia.

In a few hours, thousands of videos had been posted on the Net, triggering an outpouring of emotion and of solidarity that had never been witnessed before in the history of humankind. For the first time perhaps, humanity was taking the pulse of its collective dimension on a planetary scale. Once again, a distant event for many, helped a huge number of people change their perception of the world.

At this point, some of you might think that I always happen to be in the wrong place at the wrong time. But mind you, I wasn't in Japan on 11th April 2011! That day saw a powerful earthquake followed by a dreadful tsunami. People were able to follow live from a helicopter the humongous wave. This event too was to unleash a feeling of immediacy and closeness and often of collective and planetary fear. In that year of the Fukushima disaster, my neighbor in Ardèche (South of France) decided not to prepare a vegetable garden for fear of the after-effects of radioactivity on her crop! All the internet sites selling Iodine tablets were stormed and went very quickly out of stock in the USA and the world at large. Geiger counters sales exploded.

In all these instances, the Internet was an amazing catalyst for spreading this feeling of belonging to the same human community. It also became an irreplaceable means for getting news of one's near and loved ones or to mobilize the financial aid that helped assuage, at least to some extent, the effects of those dramatic events.

And it was above all, for most of us living on another part of the planet, an event that impacted the whole world and our lives and emotions and actions almost in real time.

Over 2.5 billion people have access to the Internet. Over 5 billion have a mobile phone, 6 according to others estimations, which itself is increasingly connected to the

Internet. There are, consequently, more people who have a mobile than who have a bank account. There are also more people on the earth who have a mobile than those who have access to drinking water or toilets.

Even if one were to question the accuracy of these figures, none can deny that information is moving faster and faster and becoming more and more significant between the different sections of society and different parts of the world. Events that were once isolated can now be linked up at great speed. This increases the role of transmission and magnifies the changes taking place.

Summing up: the population of the earth has doubled in 40 years, half of the world's population live in cities, and they are all connected to one another.

> One day you read that terrible floods are taking place in Thailand. Just a few weeks later, you decide to replace the hard disk of your computer and realize that in your favorite local shop, the prices for hard disks have gone up by 30 percent. What's the connection with the floods, you may ask? Well, this is how we found out at the end of 2011 that most hard-disk manufacturers in the world get them made either wholly or partly, in and around Bangkok and that the floods had nearly halted their supply in the world market!

We have gone from an uncertainty that was local to an uncertainty that is global. We were at one time subjected only to our local uncertainties. When there was a flood in Thailand, it was the Thais' problem, not ours. If there were possible consequences for us, by the time they reached us they had ceased to be an uncertainty. But these days in a globalized and interconnected world, a flood in Thailand leads to an instantaneous increase in the price of a hard disk at your local computer hardware retailer. The uncertainty of the Thais has become ours as well.

If we argue that the uncertainty on the planet today isn't more than before, at least we are subjected to it much more in our personal and professional lives because of its 'globalization'. We shall also see how these uncertainties form one of the components of what we will call a turbulent and chaotic world.

What is important is not so much the exact figures but rather the basic increase in the number and complexity of interactions between people. We have reached a degree of complexity in our interactions previously quite unknown in the whole of human history. It is this complexity that explains to a large extent the emergence of turbulent, chaotic workings in our civilization, as we shall see in the second part. And our vision of this civilization, which is still bogged down in our old ways of perception, which were no doubt perfectly adapted to the previous world, does not enable us to understand the phenomena of the new world.

The chaos of information

First of all, it is important to understand how the unfolding of time and the increasing number of people trigger mechanically a growth in the volume of information, regardless of the tools being used.

At the very beginning of the universe there was very little information going round. There was still very little information before life appeared on earth. This is similar to what happens to an adult who possesses more information than a child does, not merely information collected from others and from his environment but also information he has himself generated.

We can finally add that the further a system is from equilibrium – and the system we're talking about here is humankind –, the more unstable it is and the more it generates information. Actually, when a system is stable or close to equilibrium, little information is needed to describe it ("Bruno is in Paris"). The quantity of information increases when the system starts fluctuating but it remains quite limited ("Bruno is in Paris or he is in Ardèche"). However, the quantity of information increases considerably when the system loses its equilibrium and becomes unstable ("Bruno is in Paris, then in Ardèche, then in New York, then in Los Angeles, then Hong Kong, then... then...")

We can not only state that the level of information in the universe is, in absolute terms, more significant than it was a few billion years ago and continues to grow, but also that the quantity of information accessible to man is expanding. A simple Internet connection gives us access to a volume of information that exceeds the human dimension.

And so, the increase in the number of people on the earth and the increase in the degree of connectivity between them contribute to the creation of a veritable chaos of information. Today, humanity generates as much information in two days that it possibly did in 2 million years. The ex-CEO of Google, Eric Schmidt, reckoned that in 2010, we produced approximately 5 exaoctets (just remember that it's a lot) of information every two days… which is as much as was produced from the beginning of human civilization to 2003! According to the IDC institute, 1.8 zettaoctet (it is much more) of information was created in 2011. The information available on the surface of our planet in 2020 will be around 40 Zo. Every minute, about 350,000 tweets, 15 million texts and 200 million mails are sent worldwide. During the same period, tens of hours of video are uploaded on YouTube, and hundreds of thousands of files are stored on Facebook servers.

Incidentally, it is quite interesting to note that by the time I completed my initial research, I write, re-read and publish this book, these figures kept moving spectacularly upward at each stage...

In 2011, Serguei Brin, one of the founders of Google, noted that every minute 15 hours of video are uploaded on YouTube, it reached 20 hours in 2012 – that is, three years of content is uploaded each day! How much will it rise when you hold this book in your hands?

Has the world gone mad?

Let's say rather, as we are beginning to see, that it has lost its equilibrium.

We have seen in the preceding paragraphs that the increase in the number of people on earth, the increase in the number of connections, and the increase in speed, leads to what the scientists call a non-linear, turbulent or chaotic state that we shall describe in more detail in the second part of the book. For centuries, humanity has been like a pendulum at equilibrium. At times it oscillated, and then constantly regained its balance. Today the pendulum is out of balance. Not only it oscillates, it is subjected to a ceaseless movement that seems to us mad, completely pell-mell, swinging between extremes getting further away from equilibrium.

Humanity is thus faced with increasingly extreme situations, especially in the social and economic spheres and, in the long-term even more appalling, in the sphere of ecology. This is what we more commonly call a crisis. Needless to say we are going through a period of financial, economic, social and ecological crisis. These are crises that feed one another and provoke a systemic dysfunction where one pulls another down, which in turn exacerbates the preceding condition and on it goes in a vicious infernal circle. A 'poly-crisis' to use a term coined by Edgar Morin.

Let's look at some examples that show that humanity has fallen out of the state of equilibrium, examples indicating that the extremities are moving further away from equilibrium. Examples that also show us how crises multiply and amplify.

The energy crisis

The world we live in, our economies, our daily lives, basically rest on two things: cheap fossil energy and finance. It is therefore not surprising that they are the first to be affected by the crisis.

When future historians look at the last 150 years (and the next 10, 20 or 30?) they will call this the 'petrol-age', in the same way that earlier periods were qualified as the stone-age or the iron-age. We are addicted to cheap energy. I am quite aware how much the term 'cheap energy' must shock an entire segment of the world's population that can barely pay for the petrol to take them to work. Fossil energies have an apparent cost-return ratio that is unequalled in human history – obviously not taking into account the cost of pollution and other ecological consequences, nor the side effects called 'externalities'.

Most human beings, like drug-addicts suffering from withdrawal symptoms, still find it hard to accept the inevitable need for urgently shifting to an alternative energy. We shall look into some solutions for the energy sector in the third part of the book.

We'll go through some ups and downs in the cost of energy before this indispensable and inevitable shift happens. Energy-costs will continue to rise and they will do so in a turbulent and chaotic manner, buffeted by economic and political crisis. So, even as I'm writing, the USA is becoming the biggest producer of fossil energy (for how much longer?) essentially on the back of shale gas. As a result, the price of fossil energy there is among the lowest in recent history. However, this has happened at the cost of grave short-term consequences on the drilling sites, and in the long-run, even more serious consequences on the whole planet. This merely prolongs the illusory dream of cheap fossil energy… until the next ecological disaster or a war somewhere on the planet will send the prices up again.

Financial crisis

On 6th May 2010 between 2:42 and 2:52 in the afternoon at the New York Stock Exchange, the Dow Jones Industrial Average index lost almost 998.52 points before regaining 600 points. This 9.2 percent loss in ten minutes was unprecedented. Approximately 20,000 orders on 300 companies were executed at prices that were higher or lower by 60 percent of their value just a few seconds earlier. No stock operator could figure out what had happened. A mad trader? A computer blip? Manipulation?

The New York Stock Exchange's regulatory body, the SEC, explained that what has since been named 'Flash Crash' was caused by High Frequency Trading in stocks we mentioned above and which, I recall, accounts for up to two-thirds of the buying/selling operations on the NYSE.

Today mini Flash Crashes take place on a regular basis. The fragmentation of the markets into so many stock exchanges (13 organized Stock Exchanges) more or less under control is another factor. When will the 'Big One' happen?

Less than two or three percent of 3200 Billion US dollars transacted daily involves a real exchange of goods or services, the rest is all speculation. What's more, a growingly significant part of these transactions takes place outside the stock exchanges, that is to say, outside any sort of control. Thus there are 30 "Dark Pools", or "shadow" stock-markets just in the USA. These are spaces where stocks get swapped without hardly any checks and the operations mostly happen at a speed that is hard to conceive.

The financial system has become the bulwark of our economies, representing over ten percent of the GDP in the USA and Great Britain. It has become intrinsically unstable, turbulent and chaotic. It is irremediably in crisis.

Social crisis

One evening in Bangalore, I was having dinner with the head of the Confederation of Indian Industries and his wife at the very exclusive Bangalore Club, a throwback to the British colonial 'Raj'. We were talking about the way the world was changing. The gentleman remarked at one point: "The biggest problem of our times is when people who have everything meet those who have nothing." "But didn't rich maharajas always co-exist with very poor people?" I asked. "Yes, but earlier they did not meet or very little! The poor never witnessed the incredible wealth of the affluent on a daily basis. Today, all they need to do is to switch on the television or go to a mall and see a pair of sneakers they will never be able to buy. A moment will come when they tell themselves, "Why not me?" and then it'll all explode!" This was the president of the Confederation of Indian Industries talking, not a leader of the Indian Communist Party!

Between 2000 and 2010 in the USA, the economic powerhouse of the world, the number of poor went up from 31.6 to 46.2 million and the poverty ratio rose from 11.3 percent to 15.1 percent. This adds up to almost 50 million Americans who take recourse to "food stamps" in order to feed themselves and their families.

In the same period, over 20 Ferraris were sold each day (including holidays!) in the world. This was their strongest showing since the brand came into existence (in 1929 – what an irony of history!) This was true also for Rolls Royce as for the entire luxury industry in general.

Here are some more examples of a system that has gone out of equilibrium:

- Three persons have the same revenue as 48 of the poorest nations put together, and the fortune of 225 persons is equivalent to the sum total of the revenue of 2.5 billion people.

- In 2010, that is, hardly one year after one of the biggest financial crises experienced by humanity, the sum total of bonuses paid to the entire staff of the banks on Wall Street rose to $140 billion.

- For the more fortunate of the planet, the crisis is hardly a problem: in 2013, there were 1426 billionaires, which is 200 more than in 2012. This is an absolute record for the last 26 years that this classification has existed. All together, these super-rich are worth $5400 billion against $4600 billion last year, according to Forbes.

- If these billionaires were taxed 1 percent, it would raise 50 billion $.

- 3000 Americans renounce their nationality each year so as not to pay taxes in the USA.

- Military expenditure is between 800 and 1000 billion $...

- Just the maintenance of nuclear arsenals on the planet costs approximately 70 billion a year.

- Advertising expenditure is estimated at 700 billion $ a year.

These mind-boggling figures may not mean much to you. So, know that the UNO (whose budget is 13 billion $) and the principal NGOs agree on the assumption that about

US$ 100 billion would be needed to eradicate hunger, provide drinking water, basic health care, education and decent housing to all human beings. This shows the choices we make and our collective priorities...

Ecological crisis

The ecological crises are the most serious because of their short-term consequences but also and especially because of their long-term ones for our children's future.

Pollution, the accelerating extinction of animal and vegetal species, the destruction of ecological balance at different levels and as more and more people are becoming aware of this, the planet Earth, our planet and home, the only one we have so far, is in very serious trouble.

Global warming is probably one of the greatest dangers in the long-term among many others. Its consequences are difficult to foresee and potentially incalculably tragic. Man has succeeded in getting our economies, our social organizations, our political systems out of balance. If man succeeds in getting the eco-systems out of balance and renders them turbulent and chaotic, especially as regards the temperature of the planet, the consequences will be of another magnitude. And if almost the entire fraternity of scientists, minus a few light-minded skeptics still sunk in the first phase of denial, is agreed on climatic warming taking place mainly on account of human activity, we have just not been able to come to some unanimity as regards how to contain these serious effects of global warming.

We are then the first generation of humans that will pass on to future ones (our own children!) and in full awareness of consequences, a planet in a far worse shape. With no guarantee at all for their survival, and all this because of our own actions. Let's never forget that it is we who, individually and collectively, choose the world to be what it is and to a large extent what it will be for our children in the future.

In short: the situation is bad!

Humanity is at a turning-point. We are at a period when we must totally redefine the norms and values in fields not only related to work, to the economy but also to social life and relations between countries.

It is perhaps time to put on the right lenses to understand this. It is perhaps time to get the right tools so as to construct a world ever turbulent and chaotic no doubt, but also more sustainable and harmonious.

Part Two

**Acquiring the right lenses
and the right tools**

> *Fractal geometry is a
> new language. When you
> learn to speak this
> language, you can
> describe the form of a
> cloud as precisely as an
> architect can describe a
> house.*
>
> *Michael Bamsley*

Acquiring the right lenses

Japanese automobiles began flooding American roads at the beginning of the 1980s. It reached such a point that the all-powerful American car manufacturers got jittery. Japanese cars were often better-equipped, more economical to run and above all much cheaper for the buyer. When this situation started becoming seriously worrisome for the Americans, several important American car-manufacturers decided to go and check out for themselves how their rivals worked in Japan. They were warmly welcomed and the Japanese took them around several of their factories.

On returning to the USA, when they were asked by a journalist if they had discovered their rivals' secret, one of the American CEOs responded: "They hoodwinked us! We were shown fake factories! I have been in this business for 30 years and I goddamn know that you just can't have a factory without any stocks. Well, there was NO stock of any kind in their factories. I tell you it was all one big set-up, we were completely hoodwinked!"

We see the world only in terms of the ability we have to see it: the American CEOs were simply not capable of seeing a factory run without any stocks. They had been shown real factories, though, but without any stock, and there lay one of the secrets of Japanese car-manufacturing which they just could not see: no stock in the factories! Had they been capable of seeing this other reality, they could have studied it, tried to understand it and even taken inspiration from it. They did do this, but many years later, when they realized the advantage of the 'Just In Time' production strategy.

> Much prior to this, when the first Spanish Conquistadors arrived in South America on their ships, legend tells us that the Indians did not notice the ships. Very simply because they were not ready to see a large shape floating on water! They were not ready to see ships and they did not see them. It is also said that it was the shamans who first noticed these ships.

History does not tell us whether children too were able to see them. If that were true, it would hardly be surprising...

Our beliefs, our habits are veritable filters, lenses which enable us to see, to analyze, to understand the world around us. These beliefs, these paradigms, these lenses that once helped us to see the world, no longer do so because the world has changed much too fast and these lenses are no longer adapted to this fast-changing world. We are no longer capable of seeing factories exist without any stock. Like the Indians we do not see the boats sail in.

Among the lenses or paradigms we use to perceive and understand the world, three have held a very important place over time: spirituality or religions, philosophy and science. If for centuries religion had been predominant, in the last 200 years science has taken the upper hand. To such a degree that it has almost wiped out the other two. And so if science plays such an important role in the way we see and understand the world today, the least we could do is verify that our scientific 'lenses' are up-to-date!

Well, these scientific lenses are perfectly adapted to a world that is stable, close to equilibrium or that at least does not veer too far from it. They are also adapted to a binary world; right/wrong, good/bad, true/false, etc. But, as we have begun to see, the world is no longer stable. It has swung out of equilibrium and, in quite a number of domains, it has become turbulent and chaotic. It is also necessary to give up a systematically linear, binary vision and it is indispensable today to develop a vision that is adapted to a turbulent and chaotic world. For this, I suggest that we first understand how our vision of the world is connected, from among other things, with the scientific paradigm of each era. To do so, let's focus on the main scientific revolutions.

It is difficult to find the starting date and I therefore suggest that the beginning of the technical and scientific adventure was the invention of the wheel. We could date this to about 5000 years ago. We see with the wheel, in fact, how great scientific revolutions sometimes take time to be understood and become widespread, since it has taken us almost 5000 years to fix them on to our suitcases!

First revolution: how long does it take to fill your bathtub?

The first major scientific revolution was, without the slightest doubt, led by Newton who gave us what came to be called classical mechanics. With Newton, we discover that nature is comprehensible. It is also predictable. One of the basic points of classical mechanics is that if one knows the state of a system (positions and speed of the different points) at the initial moment, then one can calculate how this state will evolve in time and, therefore, determine its state at any other moment in time. That is also why we speak of a 'deterministic' vision. So, if we know the conditions at the starting-point, we will be able to predict the changes this system will go through with certainty. The cosmos is a huge machine of which it is possible to foresee all the aspects, all the transformations, all the changes in absolute time and space.

The principles of classical Newtonian mechanics are even today the principal paradigm, the main lenses we use to understand the world. And we must acknowledge the fact that we have nothing better today than classical mechanics to determine the time it takes to fill a bathtub or when two trains will cross each other. Most of us are quite comfortable with its basic principles, especially those who still have kids going to school!

So classical mechanics is perfectly suited to analyze, understand and act upon phenomena in equilibrium or close to it. It helps us, for instance, to understand the different forces at work when we study a table resting on the ground (in equilibrium). It will also enable us to understand an oscillating system that is close to equilibrium, a pendulum for example.

We can notice in a number of expressions that we use in our current vocabulary that our vision of the world is influenced by it:

- "I've found the right balance"
- "He's unbalanced"
- "It has always been like this and it won't change now"
- "All this is cyclical, it will come back"
- "It's like in 1929, in 1940, etc."
- "The pendulum will swing back!"
- "The wheel has come full circle!"

Second revolution: all is relative!

A little over a hundred years ago, two revolutions of scientific thought took place within a few years of each other: relativity and quantum mechanics.

Einstein's Relativity was the second major revolution after Newton's. Astonishing things emerged on the horizon: nothing can travel faster than the speed of light, the more we approach the speed of light, the slower time gets. The sun curves the rays of light. Nothing can come out of a black hole and so forth. And most significant of all, space and time are not absolute any more, as Newton had affirmed. They are interconnected and can alter according to the observer. Space and time are not absolute, they are relative!

Einstein had become more famous than a rock star. Even those who did not quite understand his theories of special relativity or of general relativity understand that the world will no longer be the same as before. The lenses have irreversibly changed and the consequences of this will sometimes go beyond the scientific fields. And there too, the man on the street seizes on what he has understood or thinks he has understood of the theories of relativity and uses it in his daily discourse, with expressions like: "All is relative."

Third revolution: a quantum leap

At about the same time (and what a time!) a third revolution took place in scientific thought with Heisenberg, Planck, Bohr, de Broglie, Born, Schrödinger, and others who set off what would henceforth be known as quantum mechanics. More and more astonishing things emerge for the lay man. For example, we learn that light could be either a wave or a particle. Or again, contrary to classical deterministic mechanics, that it is impossible to know at the same time both the speed and the position of a given object. Or yet again, the probability that I could go through a wall without any damage to me or to the wall is not zero. This is not to encourage you to attempt this at home for the probability isn't very high really.

It marks the entry of probabilities into what was earlier a deterministic world. It is impossible to foresee precisely when and how certain phenomena will occur. We can only know the probability. Relativity was already a revolution of thinking but at least it was polite enough to maintain the rule of cause and effect. Quantum mechanics questions this and partially turns it upside down. It isn't only quantum mechanics that partially challenges it. Chance makes its cheeky entry on the scene. Another wall of classical thinking crumbles and once more, it is translated in our everyday language with expressions like: "It's a real quantum leap!"

Why the chaos theories are important for you?

Linear mechanics could be said to be at a human scale. It allows us to analyze systems and phenomena that are not too different from the human scale: neither too small nor too large. In very small and very large cases, we'll realize that it does not hold any longer. Classical linear mechanics is thus perfectly suited to analyze phenomena at the human scale, to understand and act upon a world in equilibrium or close to it. The lenses offered to us by classical Newtonian mechanics suited us perfectly as long as we were few on earth and without much communication compared with today. We shall see that if Newtonian mechanics is ideal for understanding systems and phenomena that are in equilibrium or that oscillate yet remain close to equilibrium, it is not at all ideal in today's turbulent and chaotic world.

Moreover, we observe that relativity and quantum mechanics do not handle phenomena at a human scale. And most of us, I feel, are still quite far from understanding these notions. Relativity basically deals with what is very, very big and very, very fast. So unless you travel at the speed of light or live close to a black hole, which is hardly commonplace for most of us, the new lenses brought by Einstein, however important they might be to science or from a philosophical and spiritual standpoint, will not necessarily change the understanding of our daily lives. It needs to be noted, however, that the indirect consequences are real enough – take the cases of energy and nuclear weapons, for example.

One could simplify by saying that the theory of relativity is less relevant at the human scale rather than at the scale of the infinitely large or the infinitely fast.

As for quantum mechanics, it deals with the very, very small. And the lenses it brings, important as they might be from the philosophical and spiritual standpoint, will not, for that matter, change the understanding of our daily lives. As for relativity, we are quite clearly there are very few who understand fully its concepts. This is of no importance as its direct consequences are not so significant in our daily lives today even though its indirect consequences are beginning to seem important, with the transistor, laser, etc.

One could simplify by saying that at the human scale the theories of quantum mechanics apply little; they apply more at the level of the infinitely small.

The importance of the theory of chaos

David Ruelle, one of the first scientists to speak about the theories of chaos, writes: "The more oscillators there are and the more interconnection there is between them, the readier we should be to see chaos." We saw in the first part of the book that the increase in the number of persons on the planet (the oscillators) and their interconnections (they are coupled) causes turbulence and chaos. The world is no longer in equilibrium and is veering away from it faster and faster in numerous fields. And this not at the infinitely large or the infinitely small scale but at the human scale!

We shall also see how the theories of chaos give us new lenses and new tools to handle the turbulent and chaotic world around us. They will help us to understand, accept and utilize the growing uncertainty of our everyday life. In fact, the theories of chaos are applicable both to the infinitely small and to the infinitely big – and especially to the human scale which, after all, is what interests us most! This is why we cannot this time around miss the philosophic and practical consequences they may have on our vision of the world, on our lives or on our organizations.

Who can believe that we can understand the new world without new tools?

Who can believe that we can create a new world without new tools?

So I propose to update you, as I would for a computer, on your Operating System! Imagine what your life would be if you had a tool to help you make sense of events that you are bombarded with on a daily basis by the press, radio,

TV and Internet and which seemingly makes no sense. Imagine having the keys to decide in your best interests the professional career to choose, the life-style choice to make, the best education to give your children, advice on your investments, etc.

Well, then, let's get going!

Fourth revolution: the theories of chaos

The last and most recent major scientific revolution is the theory of chaos, of turbulent systems, of nonlinear systems or phenomenon.

It is difficult to date the theory of chaos precisely. We know when the word 'fractal' was coined by Mandelbrot, we know that Poincarré had earlier observed several pieces of the puzzle as had Maxwell and even Einstein. So when these new discoveries in the field of chaos theory emerged, few people were able to make the connection between these attempts. Mathematicians understood a discovery in mathematics, physicists in physics, meteorologists in meteorology, etc.

Thus it is difficult to attribute the theory of chaos to any single person as we do for classical mechanics (Newton) or for relativity (Einstein), or to a few scientists for quantum mechanics. As far as the theories of chaos are concerned, it's hard to focus on a certain person or persons, a certain place or a precise time, or even a common scientific field. We have people like Poincarré, Lorenz, Feigenbaum, Yorke, Ruelle, Mandelbrot, Prigogine, etc. conducting research in fields as varied and as distant as mathematics, physics, meteorology, finance, hydraulics and biology.

In order to see the emerging coherence of this thinking and its applications in the development of our vision of the world, we had to wait for real unifiers to appear, specialists of the systemic and of epistemology such as Ilya Prigogine and Isabelle Stengens, Edgar Morin, and Erwin Lazslo.

If the preceding scientific revolutions had something linear and binary (pre- and post-Newton, pre- and post-Einstein), the theory of chaos appeared more like a 'fractal' puzzle which for the last forty years or so has been falling into place and will continue to expand into other fields, as we are going to see. The theory of chaos which we may date somewhat arbitrarily to the end of the 1970s is one of the first developments in science that touches very diverse fields, including some very recent ones like the neurosciences.

The theory of chaos is sometimes called the "theory of non-linear phenomena", a term I shall use to clearly differentiate simple clear-cut linear phenomena from non-linear ones which have complex boundaries like fractal images that will be described a little further on.

This book does not aim to turn you into experts on the theories of chaos. I invite the most passionate of you to refer to the bibliography at the end of this book to go further and deeper into the subject.Here I propose to focus on whatever might serve as lenses or tools to help us see, understand and act upon the complex, turbulent, chaotic, fast-changing world we described earlier. We shall then zoom in on two aspects of the theories of chaos: the evolution of chaotic systems and the fractal images.

The evolution of chaotic systems

Isaac Asimov, the visionary science-fiction writer, recounts in one of his short stories[1] the narrative of a people that from generation to generation, from one civilization to the next, ask a gigantic computer: "Will we be capable one day of beating the second law of thermodynamics?" And for generations on end, century after century, the computer systematically gives the same answer: "Data insufficient to answer question." Billions of years pass, stars and galaxies die but the computer connected directly to the energy of Space-Time, continues to calculate. At the end, the universe dies but the computer finally comes to a conclusive answer. He now knows how to beat the second law – and that is when a new universe comes into being.

Entropy reigns and nothing can escape the implacable hold of the second law of thermodynamics. This is what we learned at school: with every passing second our world, our solar system, our entire galaxy come progressively closer to their inevitable death at the end of Time. Disorder will only grow. "And to dust you shall return."

The theories of chaos teach us that all this is but one facet of history! They do not challenge the second law of thermodynamics. They do not deny that all shall return to dust but they show us the emergence of an incredible complexity ever since the universe began. At the dawn of time, when we thought only the void existed, matter emerged, followed by life and then consciousness. The

---

[1] ASIMOV Isaac, *The last question* in *Robot dream*, Ace Books, 1956.

universe has not stopped growing in complexity nor has it ceased to evolve. Man and humanity have done the same

From atoms to molecules, from unicellular organisms to multicellular ones, from the reptilian brain to the brain of mammals until we arrive at the neocortex in man, the universe has not ceased to surprise us with its inexhaustible creativity. Continually integrating the already existing in order to grow in complexity and evolve, passing from the mineral and life to a greater consciousness, to more beauty, truth and goodness. Evolution, self-organization, integration – that is the other facet of history.

We are living at a unique moment in which humanity, itself the product of billions of years of evolution, suddenly has become conscious of this evolutionary process.

The theories of chaos bring to us absolutely essential elements to understand how we can help in this growth towards increasing complexity. (Any volunteers for a return to death and dust?) They show us how a system can evolve towards either greater entropy or towards greater complexity. They also enable us, thanks to a radically new way of seeing, to observe and take part in this evolution. For the first time in human history man has become conscious that he is not merely a spectator but also an actor in the evolution of the universe.

Let us come down from the stars then and look at one of the classic examples used in the theories of chaos to understand the evolution of turbulent or chaotic systems: water flowing out of a tap. Do the experiment at home. (It would be more clearly visible with a river but then that would be a little bothersome to do in an apartment!)

If you open a tap very gently, you will get a regular, steady, seemingly immobile flow called a stationary, linear, laminary flow. If you keep opening the tap very, very slowly you might notice a regular, subtle pulsation of the water jet. This is the 'oscillating' or 'periodic' state. If you keep opening the tap further, the pulsation becomes irregular; then, opening it even more, the flow becomes downright turbulent. Open the tap even further. At a certain point the water jet becomes a torrent. This is the turbulent or chaotic state – total chaos! But don't stop there! If you keep increasing the release of water, a surprising phenomenon can occur. Swirls might appear. Order is now emerging from chaos, order from disorder!

We can illustrate these phenomena in a simplified manner with the following diagram:

A system may be stable, in equilibrium: it doesn't move, it doesn't evolve.

System at equilibrium represented here by a straight line

Then after a certain moment, the system may start oscillating like the tap water described above or like a swing. That is represented by a sine curve in the diagrams above.

System oscillating

In this condition the system is still under some sort of control, there are some effects from 'negative feedback'. It's like a thermostat. If the heat crosses a certain temperature, the heating is cut off. Likewise, if the temperature decreases a little too much, the heating switches on.

At a certain threshold called the "Tipping Point", the system can go out of equilibrium. The oscillations keep increasing after that.

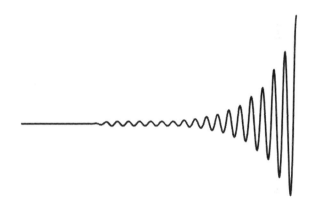

System going out of equilibrium after the 'Tipping Point'

And the theories of chaos teach us that once that point is crossed, the system will never be able to regain its previous equilibrium. This is due to the effects of 'positive feedback'. The phenomenon is self-amplified. The higher the temperature, the more we raise the heating. There are numerous examples of positive feedback in physical, biological and social systems. There is positive feedback when we are born: the pressure of the baby's head on the uterine neck triggers the uterine contractions. The contractions push the head further into the uterine neck, which in turn multiplies the contractions further. Positive feedback then leads to the expulsion of the baby from the womb. And here we are a few years later writing or reading books on the future of the world!

Let us turn our attention to the creation of social networks like Facebook. If few people use it, then few people want to join it. On the other hand, if you have more friends who use it, then the temptation is greater to subscribe to it. The more people use it, the more other people want to use it, and so it goes.

Positive feedback then is an accentuation, an amplification, an acceleration of a process by itself on itself: demographic growth, thermonuclear reaction, capital deposited on compound interest, economic depression, panic in a crowd, etc. In everyday language, we also talk about a vicious or a virtuous circle, based on whether we like the acceleration of effects or not.

What happens post-equilibrium, after the oscillations, after coming out of a state of equilibrium, called the 'decisive point'? Two possibilities emerge: either the system collapses – this is the working of the second law of thermodynamics: "And to dust all shall return":

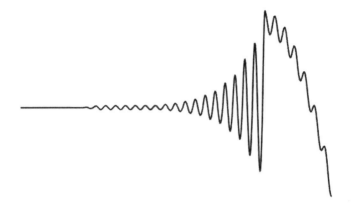

Breakdown after the 'decision point'

or there is a breakthrough, and the system finds a new equilibrium at a higher level of complexity.

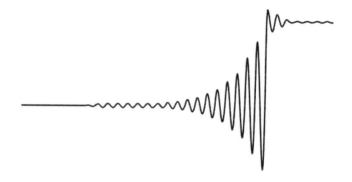

Breakthrough after the 'decision point'

This is how the living and the universe have evolved as we described earlier: from atoms to molecules, from unicellular organisms to multicellular ones, from the reptilian brain to the brain of mammals, until we arrive at the neocortex in man. The system continues to integrate what was there earlier and self-organizes in order to grow in complexity.

Most people, interestingly, find a negative connotation in the words *chaos* and *turbulent*. "It's pure chaos" or "what a turbulent child" are rarely used as compliments. But aren't these words merely a description of a state of things – neither good nor bad? Just as water can be in a gaseous (steam), liquid or solid state (ice), a collection of elements or a system can be in a state of equilibrium, linear, oscillating or even turbulent and chaotic. We can thus look at the turbulent or chaotic state as a specific phase of a system. As the material which can be in gaseous, liquid or solid phase, system can be a linear phase, oscillating or chaotic. We shall see further that what we define as a 'system' is applicable also to human beings, to our organizations, to our companies and to humanity as a whole.

We are talking then about dealing with a system using the appropriate tools to the phase it is in. Several aspects of humanity and of our organizations are still linear or in a state of equilibrium. We shall thus use classical mechanics to understand and act upon such a system. However, as we saw in the first part of this book, humanity has come out of the state of equilibrium in a number of fields and has entered a turbulent and chaotic phase. Therefore, using the theories of chaos we shall try to develop new tools, new lenses in order to clearly see the ships, the stockless factories, the 'weak signals.' We will thus be able to understand and, most importantly, to act upon those parts of our personal lives, of our organizations and of humanity that have entered a chaotic phase. We will be able to see and understand the different developments, the crisis, and work towards the emergence of new equilibriums and more complex and harmonious organizations. We will then be able to choose to work towards this emergence or breakthrough and not merely be victims of a collapse or breakdown.

This shall be our endeavor in the following pages. But before that, let us look at a second tool that the theories of chaos offer us to understand and act upon this fast-changing world: fractal images.

What is a Fractal?

How to see this emergence or breakthrough? How to reconcile two extremes that are often incompatible? Here again, one needs to change lenses, by renouncing too simplistic a vision, one that is too binary and linear. And for this, I offer you a second tool out of the theories of chaos: fractal images. For, they will help us to recognize the instances of emergence in a new world.

The term 'fractal' was used for the first time by Benoit Mandelbrot. This is how he defined fractals: "Fractals are objects, whether mathematical, created by nature or by man, that are called irregular, rough, porous or fragmented and which possess these properties at any scale. That is to say they have the same shape, whether seen from close or from far."

To understand the difference between classical and fractal geometry, look take the difference between the blade of a knife and the coast of Brittany.[2] Watched under the microscope, the blade of a knife appears very irregular and full of rough edges. But if we change the scale, to the naked eye, the blade appears completely straight. On the contrary, if you look at the coast of Brittany from not too high up, you see an irregularly indented coast. But if you change the scale by increasing the altitude, you still continue to see an indented coast!

Let's linger a little longer with Brittany.

> One rainy day (!) in Brittany, while thinking of ways to occupy the three children who were

---

[2] West of France

visiting us, I thought of an interesting game: "Find out the length of the coast of Brittany. He who comes closest to the correct answer, wins a piece of Kougnamen[3]." After a short silence, the three children came back all excited at having found the right answer. The eldest of the three showed me the map of France which he had used to calculate, and announced proudly: about 260 kms. His younger brother announced that to his mind, the coast was almost its double, which is 500 kms. And in order to back up his conclusion, he showed us conscientiously his calculations made on the basis of a far more detailed map of Brittany used by trekkers. Finally, the youngest of the three announced almost disdainfully that both his elder brothers had got it completely wrong, yet again! "The coast of Brittany, in my view, he said, couldn't be measured as it is infinite in length: just ask a snail to go round all its rocks in order to realize that it is much longer than what my brothers had affirmed. My brothers think they are more intelligent just because they are bigger!"

Benoit Mandelbrot himself had asked the same question: "How long is the Brittany coast?" Quite evidently, the answer varies considerably in accordance with the altitude from which you measure it: a few hundred kilometers when seen from a satellite and several thousand, when measured with your ruler.

This is one of the aspects that made Benoit Mandelbrot adopt the term 'fractal'. Fractal as in 'fractured' but also as in 'fraction' since it describes objects that are of a 'non-

---

[3] For those not from Brittany, this is a cake that is almost like a drug: once you've had a taste of it you just can't stop eating!

integer' dimension. Classical geometry has accustomed us to objects of an integer dimension – space or volume, for instance, or the plane, the straight line and the point. Three values are sufficient to determine the position of something in space: latitude, longitude and altitude. Space is a three dimensional object. Similarly, two values are sufficient to define the position of something on a map. The plane surface is a two dimensional object. Finally, one single value enables us to define the position of something on a line: "It is at eight miles from here on the state highway". The line has just one dimension.

It is quite evident then that the Brittany coast does not exactly correspond to any of the preceding examples. Without going into details, Mandelbrot showed that we could define the Brittany coast with a non-integer number, a fraction, and this is how the term 'fractal' came to be.

But I didn't stop there. I asked the children to come back the following day, obviously only if it rained. The weather was in my favor. This time I asked them to describe what they could see when they were shown fractal images that appear on the following pages. I have mentioned the children's definition before each image, for I thought that if children could recognize and define fractal images, big children like us could do it as well!

"You make a big circle, then smaller ones next to the big one, and still smaller ones on the smaller ones, and when they become too small you make points."

Jeremy, age 6

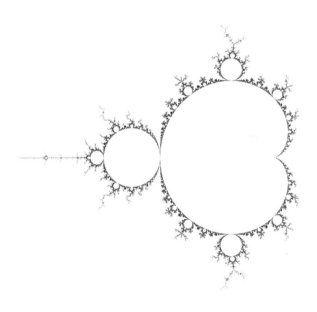

This is what is called the Mandelbrot Set or Group

"There is a cross within the cross within the cross within the cross within the cross!"

Kevin, age 7

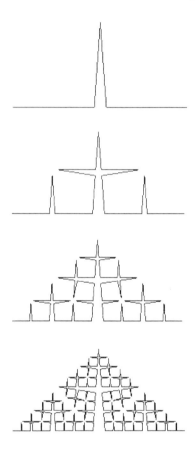

It becomes clear here how to construct a fractal image.

"You cannot measure it with a ruler; it never stops."

Bertrand, age 8

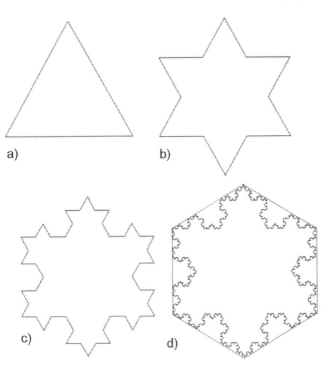

a)   b)

c)   d)

We are dealing here with the Koch snowflake.

You will notice that the outer line of the snowflake (d), though of an infinite length if we continue to increase our accuracy, fits into a limited surface. An infinite length can thus be contained within a limited surface.

"It's like a Lego with a cube that helps us to make a bigger cube that helps us to make a bigger cube that helps us to make a bigger cube."

Jeremy, age 6

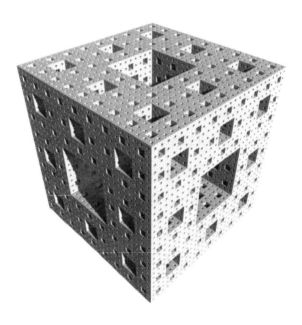

This is called the Menger sponge

"The closer you come or the further you move away, the more it is the same."

Kevin, age 7

This is the Julia Set or Group

As Mandelbrot pointed out, we see that in all these fractal images, each portion can be seen at any scale: each part is (visibly) a copy of the whole. This phenomenon is called self-similarity. A snowflake is then a marvelous example of fractals. If you see it through a magnifying glass, you see a structure with six sections. If you see one single section you observe that it too is composed of six sections. The same thing is true of a fern stalk[4] or of the romanesco cabbage.

A romanesco cabbage

---

[4] cover picture

A Patagonia tree in Argentina

A snowflake, the leaves of a tree, a cloud are a few examples that can be described through this branch of fractal mathematics. So, we can confirm that contrary to the approximations of classical geometry, clouds aren't spheres, mountains aren't cones and lightning doesn't move in a straight line. Clouds, mountains, lightning as well as trees, rivers, drying soil and galaxies, are all fractals. Nature itself is seldom linear, it is often fractal!

In the Atacama Desert in Chile

By using relatively simple mathematical formulas, mathematicians are able to create complex geometric constructions, from an infinitely small pattern which can be repeated up to the infinitely large, that reproduce nature as faithfully as possible. Not perfectly, in fact, far from it, but far more faithfully than traditional geometry did. In fact, most 3D modelisation softwares use the science of fractals in order to reproduce clouds, mountains, trees, rivers, hair, etc. The special effects in films and video games would not have had the quality they have today without fractals.

The theories of chaos teach us an important fact just as fractal images do, and that is sensitivity to initial conditions: the slightest change in the initial conditions can bring about a huge change in the end. It is almost the opposite of the deterministic vision. So it is sometimes difficult to foresee the final outcome because the smallest difference can have very significant consequences on the final result.

The union of the spermatozoon and gamete is a good example of sensitivity to initial conditions: if another spermatozoon had won, you would not be reading this book. Likewise, the slightest change, however simple, in a mathematical formula at the origin of a fractal image will lead to a completely different image at the end. Like in the phenomenon of positive feedback that we mentioned earlier. We shall refer to this again when we deal with the butterfly effect at the conclusion of the book.

The few elements we have just seen should suffice to refine the tools needed to understand the fast-changing world, as we shall see in the third part.

The world is no longer linear, it is no longer relative, it is no longer quantum – it is chaotic! Or more precisely, it is linear *and* relativistic *and* quantic *and* chaotic.

Now we will be able to recognize fractal images around us. We will be able to see ships, and see factories that run without stocks. We will be able to follow the example given to us by nature and be ready to understand that order can emerge from disorder and we can learn to manage our lives, our organizations in a more *fractal* way.

Part Three

So, what do we do?

You need to have chaos within you to give birth to a dancing star.

Friedrich Nietzsche

My aim in this third part is to show how we can apply what we have learnt from the theories of chaos to a certain number of examples, especially the evolution of turbulent and chaotic systems and fractal images. The aim is certainly not to be exhaustive but rather to get warmed up, to get ready to wear our new lenses, use our new tools in the fields of the development of individuals, of the relationships between them, of our institutions and our organizations.

But one indispensable condition before we start: out goes the binary vision!

Giving up the linear binary vision

To start with, let us see how the world has changed from quite homogenous groups with clearly defined boundaries, to a world where we find one group within another, at different scales, as in fractal images we just talked about. What is far is found sometimes near – and what is near is found sometimes far. Binary gives way to fractal. Let's take some examples:

- **The Right-Left separation in politics**: The political world was divided clearly between the Right and the Left. In certain circles, they used to vote from father to son for the same party. Of course, that might still be true today, but we also see more and more voters who vote for one party even while they openly share certain ideas of the opposing party. And so, in a presidential election, we see a candidate advocating strongly for rightism and, simultaneously, quoting a leftist iconic leader. And a leftist candidate who wishes to rally the most popular classes, but also advocates a strong and just order.

These are not just electioneering speeches; these are men and women politicians running after an electorate that is fractalising!

- **The feminine-masculine relations**: The images of man and woman were clearly defined and very distinct, often opposite. Well, today men are asked to express their femininity and women do not hesitate to affirm certain qualities that were considered masculine not long ago. Men are becoming *metrosexual*, taking great care of their appearance and exhibiting attitudes that would have classified them as homosexuals just a short time ago.

Women are not becoming masculine or men feminine, it is the masculine-feminine concept that is fractalising!

- **The world of fashion and trendsetters**: Not so long ago, a few cities like Paris, London, New York, Tokyo, boasted of "trendy" stores and dictated the new rules of fashion and trendiness to the rest of the world. For the fashionable, the rest of the world was a vast provincial no-man's land. Today, there are places that display all the codes of fashion and where we find the same public, somewhat more 'local color', in Mumbai, Bangkok and elsewhere in the world.

The world of fashion or style is not getting standardized, it is fractalising!

- **The modes of consumption**: formerly, the rich ate salmon and the poor went to hard-discount stores. Today, salmon is found at all tables, as also other fine foods earlier reserved to the upper echelons of society. The rich shop both at the delicatessen on Madison Avenue as at hard-discount stores. Similarly, airlines were accustomed to categorizing their passengers in very distinct classes: First, Business and Economy. These same airlines notice today that their customers travel First class one day and Low-cost the next. Or that the low-cost Logan automobile surpasses the expectations of Renault as more and more rich people are going for it!

It is not just the upper-crust products that are becoming available to all and the rich that are acting like the poor, it is consumer habits and reflexes that are getting fractalized!

- **Places of education and learning**: These places were extremely localized and well-demarcated mainly in the well-known university towns or the major world capitals. This is no longer so today. For instance, at the beginning of 2007, MIT (Massachusetts Institute of Technology) decided that all their courses would be available online for free. Ever since most major schools and universities have followed their example. Today, we see completely virtual universities and courses available on the Internet. So, anyone with an Internet connection has access to almost any kind of learning, while his neighbor or cousin in the countryside remains in ignorance if he is not connected.

It is not only a 'global digital divide,' this is a fractalization vis-à-vis access to knowledge and education.

I will return a little later to some of these examples, in particular to those connected with education. We shall also look at others such as consciousness, daily life, family life, geopolitical and religion, organizations and management, etc.

The one who tries to understand, analyze or predict the development in all these fields by observing them in a linear way is doomed to failure. A fractal vision alone will enable us to understand these fields, predict their development and act.

From linear/binary vision to fractal vision: when the great Asian and Western philosophies meet

We had a glimpse of this in the first part of the book. For the first time in the history of humanity, the different cultures present on our planet meet at a scale and a frequency unheard of in the past. The meeting of Western and Eastern cultures, in particular, can help us get out of linear conditioning and out of duality towards a vision that is more suitable to an increasingly turbulent, chaotic world, a vision that is more fractal!

East / West, a more fractal way of interpreting

How to go from the logic of *or* to the logic of *and*? How to make incompatible things co-exist in harmony? Western and Eastern thought have numerous differences, even oppositions. These differences and oppositions can help us to better understand the fast-changing world we have begun to perceive.

Duality / Non-duality

Duality is one of the main characteristics of the Western world-view. A thing is either true *or* false. It is good *or* bad, black *or* white, not both at once. It cannot be good and bad at the same time. You are either a singer or an actor, a politician or a humorist, etc. It is impossible to be both. You can't be in two slots at once. God is good, always good. The devil is bad, always bad. If we do not agree, it means that one of us is wrong and naturally it cannot be me – this is why there is no end to argument in a dualistic world.

Eastern thought is less dualistic, more holistic and monistic. Black *and* white can go together like the Chinese symbol of Yin and Yang:

Black and *white in the Chinese symbol Yin and Yang*

I have also understood from my Indian friends that in Hinduism, when it comes to gods, it is never very clear whether they are good or devilish.

The more scientifically savvy among you know that as science has evolved, it has moved progressively towards non-duality. First with light, which is both wave and particle at once, then the pervasiveness of non-duality in quantum mechanics, as well as nonlocality. But apart from these exceptions reserved to the scientific elite, the average citizen lives with an interpretative mode that is very much anchored in duality.

One of the characteristics then of the Eastern vision is non-duality: Yin and Yang. The world is non-dualistic – monistic – a thing can be true *and* false.

Is there a better example to illustrate non-duality than the term 'socialist market economy' used by the Chinese? Or again, the Buddhist concept of the void which roughly defined says: "All comes from the void. Therefore, the void is full."

Permanence / Impermanence

In the West, we live in a world of permanence: something that is true today will continue to be true tomorrow – and in twenty billion years as well. If it is like this today, it will be like this tomorrow and for centuries on end. On the other hand, for Buddhism which has left a strong imprint on a large part of Asia, all is impermanence. Buddha says: "There is nothing constant in the world except change." This is also true in Hinduism.

So, when His Holiness the Dalai Lama is asked about reincarnation, he always replies: "There are elements available to our understanding which make us believe in reincarnation. If you have other elements or deductive reasons that prove the non-existence of reincarnation, we can stop believing in it right away!"

Linear or cyclic time

The Western vision of time is linear. If I want to represent the passing of time with a diagram, I will draw an arrow, the arrow of time. The beginning starts with the Big Bang, it is the Genesis, and then there will be an end: the Apocalypse, Paradise. One before, one after. It is a linear way of understanding time.

Linear time is represented with an arrow

The Eastern vision of time is circular, cyclic: after spring, summer, after summer, autumn, after autumn, winter. And then it starts all over again. After one life, you have another life. After one universe, there is another universe.

Cyclic time is represented with a circle

The teleological / morphological world

The way you look at time deeply influences the way you look at life.

When you think that time is linear, then what is important is where you're going, the goal, the objective. If you do not know where you want to go, you will never reach it. The end justifies the means. You are in a teleological world – from the Greek *télos*: meaning end, goal, and *logos*: speech.

When you see time as circular, you can still have an objective. You may want, for example, a larger car, a good family, but if you fail to get one now you can succeed later, even in another life! Here, if you follow the right protocols, the right processes, you need not worry – you will reach your destination. And there is even more than this: even if you do not know where you want to go, and you don't have an objective, you need not worry either. Just follow the right processes, the right rituals and you will reach there where it is best for you to be.

When time is cyclic, what counts is not so much where you are going but how you go there. If you are walking correctly on the right path, sooner or later you will reach your goal. The means will get the ends they deserve. You are in a morphological world – from the Greek *morphé* or *morphos*, meaning form, shape.

These are two completely different ways of organizing one's life. For the West, what is important is 'the' truth and there is only one. In Asia, follow your own path which may be quite different from the path of others but follow it well!

Truth or the path

This is why Westerners attach such importance to the truth, whereas for Easterners, what is important is the path.

For example, if I tell a French person that I'm a vegetarian, his first question will be "why?" The famous search for truth... He might, of course, also ask me whether I am a vegetarian or a vegan, etc. He wants to know in which slot he can fit me. There we have duality again. An Easterner might ask me, "Since when?"

It is much easier to adapt to another form of thought (duality for instance) when you live in non-duality (everything and its opposite are possible). It is much more difficult to adapt to another form of thought (for instance non-duality) when you live in duality (I am right, you are wrong). In duality, evolution happens only through revolution (you were wrong, now we are right).

Is making a breakthrough easier in non-duality? One could accept that the concern for constant improvement can allow for a certain number of repetitions which multiplied both in time (duration) and in space (the number of people trying) could make easier the possibility of breakthrough. Evolution is easier than revolution but then it may also be slower.

It is only by integrating the two forms of thought (dual/non-dual, permanent/impermanent, linear/cyclic, etc.) that we can contribute to the advent of a new form of fractal thought. We will return to this point later in a more pragmatic way at the end of the third part when we focus on a fractal method for the resolution of the problem.

The challenge is not the Eastern vision *or* the Western vision but the Eastern *and* the Western vision. The integration of Eastern and Western thought; duality/non-duality, linear/cyclic, permanent/impermanent, truth/path, teleological/morphological cannot happen through opposition or confrontation. We are in need of union, of integration, of both the Eastern and the Western vision. This union can happen through a fractal vision, with the help of the science of chaos, of order within disorder: a complex non-duality. Our vision of the world must evolve towards a fractal duality/non-duality, a fractal Yin and Yang:

A fractal Yin and Yang

Truth, good and beauty

Let us dwell a little bit longer in the East to move into this third part of the book.

In the Japanese art of archery, Kyudo, the principal objectives of this traditional teaching are: virtue (善, zen), beauty (美, bi) and truth (真, shin).

- **Virtue** implies good, goodness. To be in a state of equanimity in the face of any event, to be detached from feelings such as envy, anger, elation, joy. The objective is to manage the inner and outer conflicts in order to achieve the right shot in archery. Such an objective is attained thanks to kindness.

- **Beauty**: Beauty is the result of movement harmonized with breathing and with the optimum economy of force. The archer does not seem to make any effort when the string is drawn.

- **Truth**: Truth is about the archetype of archery and about effortlessness in the effectuation of the shot by the archer. This becomes evident through the sound produced by the string, the bow and the impact of the arrow on the target; one feels the 'limpidity of the shot'.

In Japanese archery, as with the ancient Greek philosophers right up to Ken Wilber and Integral philosophy, we should keep in mind only one fundamental secret for interpreting the world: beauty, goodness and truth.

I suggest you use this interpretation key to observe the world and its evolution and to act in it with your new tools and your new fractal lenses. We shall, then, begin by studying the evolution of the human being and of our beliefs (beauty). We shall after that pay attention to observing the evolution of relationships between human beings and cultures (goodness). And finally, we shall see how our institutions and organizations (truth) evolve and can evolve in order to survive and develop in a turbulent and chaotic world.

Our species is evolving – and you? (Beauty)

We shall see here how the individual or each one of us can develop, evolve and blossom in a fast-changing world.

Kevin's life: how life has become fractal

Pierre and Marie are 70 and 71 today. They have two children: their son Philippe, 43 and their daughter Sophie, 39. Pierre was born in a small village near Lyon. It is in this village that he went to school up to the BEPC (French General Certificate of Secondary Education). Then he started working in a factory in a neighboring village. It was actually in his place of work that he met Marie. They have brought up their children with care and affection and they have tried to pass on the values they consider important. So, for instance they explained to them right through their childhood that working hard at school was important in order to succeed in life and not be in any want. Similarly, both of them are practicing Catholics, so they tried to transmit the essence of Christian values to their children. They live today in a house they set up over the years and in due time, they wish to be buried in the little cemetery where Pierre's parents already rest.

Pierre's and Marie's lives, a few incidents notwithstanding, have been very *linear*.

Their son Philippe left them when he was about 18, to continue his higher studies in engineering in Lyon and succeeded brilliantly. It was during a training in London that he met his wife Anna, a British Muslim of Indian origin. After a brilliant start in his career, to the great pride of his parents, he had to radically change his career after being laid off like many of his colleagues when the company was bought up by a Chinese firm. He now works in Milan where he was able to find a consultant's job. He finds it very hard to explain his professional career changes to his parents who themselves find it embarrassing to talk about it to their village friends. Their son, however, has tried to reassure them that he makes more money now as a consultant! His wife Anna stayed on in London where she holds an important post as a financial analyst in a major bank. Philippe and Anna commute on the weekends to get together either in London or Milan. Their 11-year old son Kevin studies in the International Lycée of London. He has already become used to airports and has his own Frequent Flyer Gold card!

Philippe and Anna's life is already a little less *linear*. But what will happen to Kevin's? Let's try imagining it.

Kevin is perfectly trilingual. He speaks French, English and Chinese, which he started learning on his own from the age of 8! Even though he will pursue his studies longer than his father, he will start to work very early. His study time will be punctuated by various training and learning programs. He will interrupt his studies at several points in order to spend long periods abroad, for instance in China to perfect his Chinese, but also on various humanitarian missions in different countries. During these periods, he will be paid either by his employers, either by government or by non-profit organizations. Come to think of it, it is impossible, in fact, to say for sure when Kevin will complete his studies and start a professional life.

Once he gets older, he will interrupt his 'professional' life for longish periods, either to take up some new course or to go once again on new humanitarian projects in several countries. He will also take several long breaks, which we qualify today as *holidays*, dedicated to the discovery of the world ... or of himself.

Likewise, it is very hard to say when he will retire. His life during his forties and even his fifties will continue to be punctuated by alternating activities of all kinds, either remunerated or done simply as a pastime.

Kevin, who was brought up in great religious freedom (his father is a Catholic and his mother a Muslim), will discover at the age of 16, while training in a martial art in Japan, Zen Buddhism. He will go on a number of retreats in the course of his life. If asked about his religion, he will find it hard to answer. He may even sometimes wonder whether he isn't more Eastern than Western. In any case, he will affirm that spirituality is an indispensable part of his life.

At a personal level, he will most probably marry much younger than his parents did – to their great astonishment. He will also divorce much earlier[5]; in fact, he will renounce the idea of marriage quite fast and quickly embrace the idea of a contract of living a shared life with his different partners. He will have several kids from his different partners and will be completely focused during certain parts

---

[5] When our great grandparents got married, statistically speaking, they took a vow of fidelity for only five or ten years, now it is for sixty years! We still say 'marriage', but a commitment for ten years and a commitment for sixty years isn't quite the same thing!

of his life in the education of children who are not his. For a few years, he might even live with a gay partner and be involved in the education of his gay partner's children!

He will also share not just his private life with his different partners but also his professional and associative projects. Vice versa, his partner (male or female) in a professional project is sometimes the mother of his children or his lover. It is sometimes difficult to demarcate his personal from his professional life.

Besides, they often work from home. The border between private and work space becomes difficult to define.

Kevin's life is quite clearly very fractal!

Let us see in the following paragraphs how the tools, derived from the theories of chaos as well as from the evolution of systems and fractal images, can help us understand the evolution of the human being, as much from his physical and emotional as from his spiritual point of view.

Fractal identities: Who am I?

> I met, not long ago, a very dear friend who complained to me frequently that she suffered due to the hugely annoying disparity between her personal values and those imposed by her daily professional life. But like many, she had learned to 'live with it' and got used to it. I came to know recently that she had suffered a 'burn-out' and had just spent four weeks in a hospital, all this followed by a long acute depression.

I often meet friends or even clients who complain about the 'big disparity' between what they think in their personal life, their values, and how they behave in their daily professional life. These two worlds are becoming increasingly disparate and irreconcilable. Their double identities are in conflict and this conflict often translates itself into stress, illness and depression and 'burn-out' or mental disequilibrium. A notable statistic is that one-fourth of the French are under medication with anti-depressants, tranquillizers or hypnotics!

So we play increasingly multiple roles in accordance with the audience or the circumstances before us. We also have different identities when we are face to face or when we are online. The more the world becomes complex and fractal, the more our personality itself becomes complex and fractal in order to adapt continuously and at a growing speed to current situations and encounters. So for decades we had an almost unchanging single personality, generally conditioned by our surrounding group: our family identity, for instance: the 'son of Martin' or a geographic identity, 'Highlander' or 'Frenchie' or even a professional one, 'Taylor', 'Shoemaker', 'Tanner', etc. Then we passed on to a plural identity. We are not the same at work, with our friends or with our children. We have become fractal personalities that change and adapt continuously.

We notice acceleration even in this change of our personality. Formerly, we might change our personality once or twice in our life, rarely more. Then we began changing our identity many times in a day. And now we change our personality all the time.

Our identity, our 'self' is no longer something unique, fixed, constructed by our parents or our group. Our identity is constantly under construction, practically from peer to peer, due to the increasing number of people with whom we interact in the real and the virtual world.

Life has become a multitude of plays in which each actor-spectator plays his role in a collaborative way with the other spectator-actors. And this permanent and ever-changing play looks less and less like a classical play and more and more like improvisation!

So with all these identities that are increasingly multiple and fractal, the question arises: who are we? Our personality is no longer stable; it has become chaotic! Our understanding of the evolution of chaotic systems we studied in the second part of this book fuels the thinking, and I see two possibilities:

- One, There's a 'breakdown' (a synonym for depression in English): we lose ourselves in all these identities which might oppose until conflict... and end up becoming insane or depressed. Many people affected by depression, 'burnout' and all kinds of supposed new diseases, such as 'borderline' are symbols of this personal collapse.

- Two, there is a 'breakthrough': the emergence of a new level of consciousness embodied in our multiple identities but detached from them. A growing number of 'awakened' persons, like those called 'Cultural Creative', show the possible emergence of a supra-individual identity that is both embodied in the multiple identities and detached and 'above' them. There is thus an evolution of consciousness.

And these two possibilities of either an individual breakdown or breakthrough reflect two possible directions humanity could take: breakdown or breakthrough! The different identities of humanity, the different cultures, religions and nationalities, had lived together quite independently from one another until a few centuries ago. Today, through numerous exchanges brought about by globalization, they keep intermingling in a massive permanent way. Remember the over two billion human beings who have access to the Internet, the over five billion who have a mobile and the nearly 50,000 flights that transport people all across the globe each day we mentioned in the first part.

In order to avoid a breakdown, a great worldwide 'depression' of humanity as a human collectivity, which will affect more than just the economy, and a descent into the darkness of an era of continual conflict, of social and ecological upheaval, the emergence of a new planetary consciousness becomes indispensable for the survival of humanity.

The road towards more meaning and more spirituality is no longer the luxury or the enjoyment of a few. It is no longer an entertaining New Age accessory but a question of the very survival of the individual and of humanity as a whole.

The search for the authentic being

We have seen how we move from a single identity to multiple ones and how these identities keep changing ever more quickly. And paradoxically, while these multiple, fractal identities keep coming up, it is authenticity that is sought in the other. So how can we be multiple and authentic at the same time?

Who is authentic? It is one who beyond his multiple identities has found his true self. It is one who has allowed his supra-identity to come to the fore, an identity stationed above yet in perfect resonance with his situational identity, an identity of the moment in harmony with his circumstances and his environment. This 'self', this supra-identity, is not to be seen as an object, not even as a subject, but rather as a process in perpetual unfolding, in constant construction. It is all these processes of individual creation that are unfolding for each one of us, which taken as a whole will constitute a new human and planetary consciousness. There is no risk then that each individual self will disintegrate in a collective 'we'; on the contrary, each individual seeking for identity will blend in with the larger collectivity that will arise from the diversity of each one of us. Very much like the cells of the human body that do not drown in a formless whole, but on the contrary blend in to constitute the person we are, the consciousness of humanity is being built by incorporating the multiplicity of individual beings of consciousness.

A true, authentic person is like a perfect actor who enacts at every instant the role he has to play, a role both in harmony with his consciousness as well as adapted to the situation and his audience. And when the play changes, he enacts a new role, new even while it is in resonance with his 'self' as well. He or she 'rings true' without needing to 'put on' anything. On the contrary, the non-authentic person 'rings false', like a bad actor who plays a 'circumstantial' role without any conviction. Like the actor who always plays the same role when the play has changed; he or she 'puts on', 'lays it on thick', overacts.

The person who is not authentic or true might touch your senses, but the true person, the authentic person, moves your soul.

Your brain is fractal and chaotic!

> I remember, while conducting seminars a few years ago, that I could anticipate the moment when a break was required just by observing the expression on the smokers' faces. As soon as they began feeling slightly nervous, I knew it was time for a break! Today I feel I can do the same not by observing the cigarette-addicts but the addicts of BlackBerry and smartphones. When they start looking at or fiddling with their electronic talisman in a somewhat fidgety way, I know the time for a break has come.

The new media we use, and the veritable chaos of information we described earlier, have profoundly changed our very way of thinking. As Marshall McLuhan said once, and it sounds potently relevant today: "The medium is the message." What he meant was that it is not just information and how we use it that matters. The medium itself, the technology used, will have an impact on our way of treating this information. Internet has not merely changed the type and the quantity of information we can access, it has also changed our relationship to the information and our way of treating it. Our brain has gone from a linear mode of thinking that is calm and focused to a mode that constantly adapts itself and even demands a significant mass of short bits of information that are disjointed and multi-layered. 'Zapping' has replaced the extended evenings immersed in *War and Peace*!

So without being aware of it, our brain-functioning has evolved from the linear to the cyclic and in an ever faster and even turbulent way. It has evolved from complete immersion up to a compulsive fluttering. It is interesting to note that the linear functioning of the brain and its capacity to remain focused on the same task for a long time is quite recent compared to the length of human history. The capacity of concentration is a recently acquired skill with the training of reading. Previously, during the hunter-gatherer stage, our brain was more programmed for instantaneous reactions to what we would qualify today as distraction. This distraction could indeed be a danger or, on the contrary, an opportunity, such as an opportunity to obtain food which could not be wasted at any cost. Similar to mail or information on the Net these days which we must not miss. I remember a participant in a seminar who had placed his two BlackBerries in front of him and then stubbornly refused to switch them off: "Just imagine if I get an important message", he explained to us.

From being agriculturist-breeder of learning who sought to 'cultivate' knowledge and to develop our 'culture', we have come back to the state of the hunter-gatherer of stimuli in a jungle of information! Well, in order to understand and act upon this chaotic world of today, we must be capable of being both hunters of ideas and farmers of learning. We also need to be synthesizers of concepts.

We handle as much information in a single day as we did in a lifetime not so long ago. The increase in the flow of information to our brain is of such magnitude that one could compare it to the increase in the outflow of water from the tap that becomes turbulent (an example that was mentioned in the second part of the book). The human brain is coming out of equilibrium and out of the slow evolution it was used to for thousands or millions of years. It is entering, for many of us, a chaotic phase. With the usual consequences: breakthrough or breakdown! (Breakdown and depression being synonymous in English).

What do we do in practice? We need to develop our capacity to deal with these incredibly dense inflows of information. We must learn to 'surf' ever faster and with increasing agility on these waves of information. And also we must know how to break them. We must learn all over again to walk quietly in nature and let our body and mind relax. We must know how to switch off our phone, our PC and all sorts of electronic distractions in order to immerse ourselves in a book for a few hours. We need to get back our mastery over time. We must organize it like a fractal image which will set out a beautiful picture of our schedule. An image that evolves each day, each week, each month, but stays true to the kind of life that we wish to build for ourselves and not one that is forced on us by external stimuli.

Thanks to recent discoveries in the cognitive sciences, we know today that the brain is malleable and never stops growing, not just until the onset of manhood as was believed for so long. The brain is capable of creating throughout our life new connections and new modes of functioning. For the brain too, it is important to give up its mechanistic vision. The brain is not just a machine which once set up, ceases to function as was supposed at the outset, gradually exhausting itself and falling into disuse. The brain is not simply an assembly of independent parts, each with a distinct function. Today we look upon the brain as a system in evolution which, like all systems, can be stable, in oscillation but close to equilibrium, or turbulent and chaotic. The brain is subject to ageing and can experience breakdowns, the increase of degenerative diseases is probably a consequence. That said the brain can also be a space of breakthrough, construction and reconstruction.

As Alvin Toffler reminded us; "today's illiterate are those who do not know how to learn, unlearn and relearn."

If the temptation to give up concentrated reading is great, as it is for a growing part of the population, in favor of easy access to an abundance of ever-updated information on the Net, the answer once more is in the *and* and not in the *or*. It seems, therefore, important to me to learn or to relearn to read books in a concentrated way without any distraction. It is essential, especially in periods of major changes, to know how to 'deepen' one's thinking, and for this books, no matter if made of paper or electronic, remain the best means. And it seems to me equally important to know how to rapidly scan these continual flows of information and, like a hunter on the prowl, know how to detect the key information that unveils the meaning, the 'weak signal' that will become an important trend.

We can no longer allow events to happen at the rhythm in which they happen, unless we live very far from an Internet connection... We must be able to live in serendipity by allowing events to surprise us, and also be able to take control again by organizing our time: to reserve moments of meditation and concentration, moments of 'deep' concentrated reading, and to have turbulent moments as well, when we zap along in this abundance of information. Once more, a more fractal vision of our life enables us to reconcile the irreconcilable; to control and let go, to contemplate in serenity, the necessary concentration for reading and deep knowledge, as well as the chaos of abundant information that leads to the emergence of new ideas.

The challenge today is no longer merely to accumulate knowledge in a linear, hierarchical way but also to discover and understand the emerging meaning of this constant flood of invasive information in constantly changing contexts.

The fractal being

The important stages of our personal evolution are childhood, adolescence, adulthood and old age. A linear/binary person abandons his childhood curiosity for the endless revolts and dreams of adolescence which in turn give way to the awareness and responsibility of the adult and finally the detachment and wisdom of old age sets in.

A more fractal person will assimilate and unify all these elements in a better way: curiosity, rebellion, infinite dreams, awareness, responsibility, detachment and wisdom at each moment of his or her life. The fractal being will preserve the curiosity of the child in adult life, the capacity for rebellion and indignation of youth and always aspire for the greater wisdom that comes with ripeness.

Organizing one's life fractally?

We can look into our time-table in more detail. In a linear world, the borders between work/holiday, home/abroad, private/public are very clearly demarcated. Life is organized over long periods that hardly ever overlap: we start with education, then we enter the work-phase and we end with retirement. In a world that is fractal and no longer linear, life gets organized according to patterns where very different periods of activity have to interweave. I shall try to show how one can adapt in the best way possible to this fractal world. We will then see how our life will get fractalized so that we may learn to adapt better to this new chaotic and turbulent world.

Let us study some aspects of our life and see how we can respond in a more fractal way:

Work-time / leisure-time:

- The linear version: The prevalent organization is typical of the industry-commerce era: there are long periods of work followed by more or less long periods of rest. We are in a world of duality; either this *or* that.

- The fractal version: Sometimes we agree to work during one's holidays, but we can also enjoy moments of rest during the work-period! We can fully exploit the characteristics of the creation-communication era in a society that runs on information. Going on weekends with our laptop or Smartphone we are invaded in our private space by work-related emails, but we can also shop online or organize the next holidays on the Net during working hours!

The hardest thing of course is to define clearly the limits, or rather the membranes as we shall explain a little later. It is important to distinguish the fractal image of our personal organization!

Work-space / personal life-space:

- The linear/binary version: At present we work in one space and we live in another. It is really surprising to observe that we are simply not able to put teleworking models in place. We see in this the manager's fear of losing control over the employees' work in a frighteningly fast-changing world ...

- The fractal version: We work less and less at the office and increasingly from home but also while travelling. The modern tools of communication enable us to stay connected from almost anywhere. It is no longer the space that determines the activity to be done but we ourselves who decide what we need to do wherever we are! We thus become veritable connected nomads.

Home-space / holiday-space:

- The linear/binary version: We live in a space from which we run away for holidays as soon as we can.

- The fractal version: We have already created a work-space in our living space, so now we need to make our holiday space there as well! For instance, a space where we can read quietly or even a space where we can isolate ourselves in order to meditate. Besides, we see more and more people living in two spaces rather than one. Sometimes, we do this for reasons of family (a blended family, for instance) but increasingly we do it out of choice of our place(s) of living. We also see more and more people keep a pied-à-terre in a big city and live in the countryside. Mind you, it is no more the duality of an apartment in the city where we work and a house in the country where we go for rest! The house in the city is simultaneously a meeting point for work-related meetings but also meetings around culture and friends. And the country-house has become, thanks to Internet, a real space for work.

Learning time / work time / retirement time:

- The linear/binary version: In a linear life, the different stages follow one another without really overlapping: birth, childhood, school, higher studies, job, retirement, death. We learn, then we implement, then we rest.

- The fractal version: We learn to gain knowledge in a more fractal way. We work while we are studying and we are ready to take up studies for short or long periods at any time. We give ourselves time to read. We learn to take moments off for a retreat during a time when work is the predominant activity. We participate in professional training programs and workshops for our personal development. This implies that we learn to manage our savings and expenses for our continuous learning! The management of our teaching-learning capital must be handled like our pension capital or health capital.

Salary time / job-hunting time:

- The linear/binary version: We are either salaried or unemployed. There is nothing in between and the transition between the two is abrupt.

- The fractal version: We are on a permanent job-hunt, even when we seem to think we have a stable job. Our résumé is ever ready and our address-book always updated! In fact, we are always ready to accept long or short-term missions, where even short-term missions can be integrated in a long-term professional plan. Mind you, this is not about accepting job-insecurity as a way of life but about setting up a truly new organization of work!

Working life / time for religion-spirituality:

- The linear/binary version: Today, we either believe or don't believe. And if we believe, our life is divided between moments of contemplation and moments when we almost forget our religion. We attend Mass on Sundays and we behave like an unscrupulous boss on Mondays.

- The fractal version: Don't believe, but don't doubt either! Make our own experience of spirituality or religion. Experience our own world in creation. Feel the divine in the daily activities of our life, along our path. If you meditate, learn to do shorter meditations as well as much longer ones. Learn to meditate during the short time you have while waiting for a bus. And from time to time, offer yourself a one- or two-week retreat. This is

> how you will learn to be in a state of constant
> meditation or prayer!

We shall return with numerous other examples. But in brief, one way to fractalize your life is to know how to shorten and at the same time how to prolong the different sequences of your life. For instance, learn to shorten your holidays by knowing how to 'unplug', by being able to disconnect and to re-connecting quickly. But also, from time to time, dare to take unusually long breaks from work: three months, six months, even a year or more. Go round the world as you had dreamt while a student and take along your children if you have any. That is the best gift you can give them in order to help them discover and understand this new world being born.

Living fractally means living today, and this week, and this month, a little bit of what you wish to be in ten years time or when you retire (living in a linear fashion means waiting for ten years to pass or waiting for the time of retirement). Did you offer yourself today a moment, however brief, of 'holiday', of a 'retreat'?

Living fractally means living today, this week, this month, like the child that you were. Learn to play, to be irresponsible for a few seconds... or for longer.

By progressively organizing your live in a more fractal way, you will be better equipped both to understand and to adapt to this world that appears increasingly chaotic day after day. You will no longer be mere spectator, victim adapting in the best possible way to circumstances. You will yourself become more fractal, and blend in perfectly with this new world!

You will then be actor *and* creator of this world being born!

More fractal bio-rhythms: sources of depression, illness or evolution?

Just a few decades ago, most of us were exposed to the four seasons that unfolded changelessly. Today more and more people are exposed through their travels to the four corners of the world, either for tourism or for professional reasons, to climatic variations that are utterly chaotic! We leave in the thick of winter for the other side of the globe looking for the sun and its warmth or its intense light. Similarly, more and more people expose their bodies and their minds to time-differences (shift-work) or jet-lags caused by intercontinental travel. There is more and more summer in our winters and more and more daylight in our nights…

Now, it is proven that the body and mind are particularly sensitive to variations of temperature and perhaps even more to variations of light intensity. How do our body and our mind react to these chaotic changes? Are we seeing new behavioral patterns, new diseases caused by these changes? I would not be surprised to be told that some of us are better equipped to adapt to these changes while others react to them by sinking into depression or disease.

What could be the replies to these changes, the methods by which they do not become the cause, the source of breakdown, of depression or disease, but source of physical and mental breakthrough? Are we not aggravating the chaotic effects on our health, very much like the weather which is also becoming chaotic (summer in December, winter in June…) because of climatic upheaval and various types of pollution?

As in a fractal image, where the bigger connects with the smaller, are we forcing on to nature what we force on to our body? Are we forcing on to our body what we force on to nature?

How can and how will our body and our mind adapt?

How can and how will nature, fauna and flora adapt?

I'd say here that in a general way it is important to learn to be at least attentive to the rhythm of our body and to our mind in order to respond to their expectations. So, we need to go from a general, linear, identical rhythm for the entire population of a given territory, to a healthy management of our fractal bio-rhythm by adapting our personal environment (light, temperature, food type, etc.). One method could be, for example, to fractalize our exposure to light: by making longer periods of dim light in summer or on the contrary, longer periods of luminous intensity in winter…

The other much more natural path would be to learn to re-synchronize with nature and with the planet. The mechanistic, reductionist vision of the world that has guided us up to the present has brought about a de-synchronization of human activities with regard to nature. Lights are on 24/7. We give no importance to time-differences whose consequences must absolutely be eliminated for the sake of professional efficiency or the need to make possible the cost of our holiday. We eat strawberries in winter. Employees are on shift work. From early infancy, children are taught in school to follow a rhythm that is imposed and not to listen to the rhythm suggested by their body. The race for high productivity pushes us to go against time, leading to an ever increasing consumption of energy.

It is time to re-synchronize with the earth and our eco-system. And so our professional and productive activities need to re-synchronize with nature. Like the human body that adapts and regulates its temperature according to the time of the day and according to the season, we will have to relearn to produce in accordance with the time and the season. The optimal utilization of renewable energies tells us to switch on the washing-machine when there is sun or wind. It will be the same for the production of goods and services. These will adapt to the nearly free production of energy offered by nature. The production tool will be synchronized with the sun, the wind and the energy of waves or tides. Like our biological rhythms we can reconnect with the rhythms of the planet, we can reconnect the rhythm of our industrial productions with the natural cycles of the sun, the wind, water, waves, tides, geothermic heat sources, etc. What we lose in false classical, economic productivity, we will gain a hundredfold in sustainability, in quality of life and in sociability. What we lose in the optimization of the utilization-time of production tools, we will gain in the economy of fossil energies which will continue to rise in cost. By reconnecting ourselves with the biosphere, what we lose in terms of illusory efficiency, we will gain in the opportunities of humanity's survival and in the pleasure of living together in harmony with our environment.

The digital connected tools will enable us to manage this harmonization quite easily. In fact, there should be absolutely no technological problem and the required tools are already there.

During one of my trips to a so-called under-developed country, I was greatly astonished when a friend I met there fixed a meeting with me saying "tomorrow after the rain." You can picture my perplexity at this unsettling assault on my slightly obsessive habit of demanding punctuality. (I am being nudged to remove the 'slightly'...) Today, I can imagine perfectly how to handle my need for punctuality and respect for the natural cycles: my Outlook or Google calendar could simply incorporate an 'after the rain' function that would be permanently synchronized online with the weather forecast of the place of meeting!

We pass from linear time, ever accelerating, to fractal time that harmonizes continuously with our human and natural ecosystems.

Our hunter-gatherer past teaches us how to live in harmony with the cycles of nature.

Our agriculturist-breeding past taught us to live in a world where humans are becoming more and more numerous and resources ever rarer. We have learned in this way to give up abundance and to treat nature as a resource and not as an established fact. We have learned to garden in a limited space.

Our more recent past has also enabled us to make unthinkable technological leaps that allow many of us (not all, alas!), to live better than kings and emperors lived hardly 300 years ago.

To incorporate the rhythms of nature in our personal and professional lives means also to be in resonance with human evolution in its totality. It is to find the best of our hunter-gatherer past and be like our ancestors who lived in osmosis with nature. If we can recover a little of our forgotten knowledge of that era, it would teach us, for instance, to make the optimum use of renewable energies. In the same way, if we could retrace our agriculturist-breeding knowledge, we would know how to cultivate our earth as our common heritage, our 'planetary garden'. It is by integrating all this knowledge in harmony, and not by opposing it with the extraordinary technological advances of these last 200 years, that we will succeed in our endeavor to make a new major step forward evolution in the human adventure even while preserving everything that has made these changes possible, our 'Mother-Earth'.

How to take right decisions in a chaotic world?

A world that has become increasingly turbulent and chaotic also forces us, with an ever-pressing need, to make choices. And these choices are becoming more and more difficult. In fact, how do we take the right decision when the situation is complex, and numerous factors influence the situation and these interdependent factors keep changing? How do we take a decision in a world that has become turbulent and chaotic?

There is some good and some bad news. The bad news is that in a turbulent, chaotic world no real road exists, much less a map in the classical sense. What we have is a set of 'possibles' that keep changing at every moment. The good news is that once we are able to see this set of 'possibles', which often appear as a fractal image, nothing is simpler than following its path: the right path in general is the easiest!

In order to see one's path, one must first be capable of seeing the other paths. Only then can we choose the right one. In order to see the other paths, one must be able to perceive order in disorder and see the general pattern. We must distinguish the melody emerging out of the surrounding noise. For doing this, it is important to be able to find silence within us, to let go and give up just for a while our usual thinking pattern. And once we see order emerging out of disorder, once we see the different paths and a road-map appear, we can then choose our path. Often it is the one that appears to be the easiest, the most obvious… but only on condition that we have been able to detach ourselves from our fears. If you did not sense any sort of fear, which path would you choose to walk, which path would be the most beautiful? That path is no doubt the one to take!

Do you keep asking yourself what to do with your life or simply what to do in life? Do you ask yourself the following questions: what is my dream, what would I really like to do? What would I do if I had no fear at all of the future, the fear of being in lack of the things needed for the survival of myself and my loved ones? What would I do if I was not bothered by other people's judgments and opinions? Without any hesitation, the answer to all these questions is the right one and you are facing the right path, so just take it!

And along the path, keep your common sense and a certain flexibility. The world is changing so fast that more than ever we deserve a second chance. If the path you chose did not work out, change it. You were not necessarily wrong, it is perhaps the world that has changed too fast. The right decision is one we take with the elements available to us at the moment of taking the decision.

Going further: Fractal consciousness? Fractal universe?

We can always go further with this new way of seeing the world and use it on our consciousness itself. Mind you, if subjects that are somewhat spiritual scare you, jump to the next chapter! This chapter is meant for those who already have a deeper understanding of these questions and it is not indispensable for reading the rest of the book. On the other hand, if these questions interest you, I deal here with the most innovative and provocative ideas of this book.

We have seen how one's vision of time, linear for the Westerners, cyclic for the Easterners, can influence the way we see life, death and the different states of consciousness. So for Westerners life has a beginning and an end, perhaps followed by an after-life in accordance with their beliefs: heaven or hell. On the other hand, for Easterners, every day is a new beginning. Reincarnation is one of its offshoots.

So, let us look at the different states of consciousness that we are most familiar with:

- Waking
- Sleep
- Dream

These different states of consciousness follow one another, both in a cyclic manner (Eastern vision of things) and a linear one (Western vision) in the course of a lifetime. They follow each other, in fact, in a fractal manner:

- The state of wakefulness is itself a succession of moments when one is totally conscious and moments when one is less so. For instance, we hardly remember anything of the last ten kilometers we have driven.

- The state of sleep is itself a succession of more or less conscious phases: light sleep, deep sleep, short awakenings, etc. Some remember their dreams, and even manage to control them. Others do not remember their nights at all. They don't even remember the moments when they woke up!

Can we be conscious while dreaming? Do we dream that we are conscious? Are we conscious that we are dreaming that we are conscious that perhaps we are dreaming, etc.

In fact, what we are conscious of and what we qualify as reality on one side, and dreams on the other, as what we are not even conscious of, are joined together in a fractal way.

Death itself can be considered as another state of consciousness. No doubt our physical body disappears but our soul abides. It continues to be conscious of itself (or not), until its next physical experience (the eventual reincarnation that Easterners believe in). Most of us obviously are not conscious of our death. It is a black hole. But things could be otherwise. In the same way that we are more or less conscious during our wakeful or our sleeping state, aren't we simply unconscious during our death? Is there not something during death, is there not something we are not conscious of? Death in that case would be nothing but a fold of the fractal consciousness. Just like sleep or wakefulness.

Being immortal means perhaps remaining conscious all the time including the state of consciousness called death. Becoming immortal means then being conscious in wakefulness, in sleep *and* in death. Learning to live one's death, is like learning to watch oneself fall asleep. And isn't our learning to be conscious in our sleep already a learning to be conscious beyond death?

Numerous paths have been tried and experimented with through different forms of spirituality over the centuries and are practiced by more and more people. So in the same way that we have begun learning to organize our life in a fractal way, we can perhaps learn to be conscious in a fractal way.

Are you still with me? Then let us see a little further: is the universe fractal? If so, then why?

The universe as we perceive it is probably a projection. What is a projection? For instance, a geographical map is a two-dimensional projection of the real three-dimensional world. The film that you see on your screen is also another type of projection: in 2D, or 3D on the newer screens.

The world that we see is of a few dimensions only, in principle four: the three dimensions of space and time as the fourth. But this world as we perceive it could very well be, in fact, nothing but a projection of a universe that has a number of other dimensions, perhaps an infinite number! Well, the projection of something of a larger dimension on to something of a smaller dimension creates what we may call 'folds', such as when we try to slip a very big shirt into a box that is too small for it. Try it and you'll see!

You will notice that the se folds naturally take a fractal form and perhaps this is how we can understand the fractal nature of our universe. In the same way, our life is perhaps a fold, a fold of consciousness. Indeed, the projection of a consciousness of an infinite dimension into a human dimension that is much smaller, turns our life into a fold of consciousness.

What I call learning to identify a fractal image is, in fact, being able to see a pattern in the folds, to see order in a world of chaos. In fact, on a very small section of a dress, one does not see the totality of the folds and all seems then to be flat or linear. At the worst, it rises at places or it goes down at others. We cannot see the whole landscape. But as soon as we go further away or rise in altitude, we increase the range of our vision; then the folds and the fractal nature emerge.

Our consciousness, our life are fractal. And it is by learning to widen our field of consciousness that we might be able to perceive the complete pattern and begin to figure out its sense.

The evolution of our cultures and our social relationships (Goodness)

In this part, we shall focus on how relations are changing between human beings and how our way of looking at ourselves is also changing. We shall also look at how the relations between ourselves in a much more collective sense – our cultures – can evolve towards more consciousness and harmony.

A 'fractal' love-relationship?

In the previous chapter, we saw how the human being had recently evolved and the new perspectives of changes opening out before him. But human beings rarely live in isolation. We also saw in the first part of this book that we were increasing in numbers and that our interactions are getting ever greater. So let us use our new tools, our new lenses that have come to us from the theories of chaos. In the second part, we observed how relations between human beings could evolve. Let us begin with couples.

We can classify the evolution of the relations of a couple into several phases:

- **Physical, sexual love**: in the hunter-gathering era, the essential aim of a relationship was survival, one's own and that of one's genes. This is of course also pleasure and instinct. Thus, women will choose the dominant male, most likely to protect her and ensure her survival and that of here genes. And so the male selected the most vigorous female. For more security, he even chose several. I call it physical love, for it is essentially based on the physical part of a relationship, especially the sexual. Yes, some of you might counter by saying that my knowledge of this period starts and ends with Jean-Jacques Annaud's film *Quest for Fire* and *How I ate my father* by Roy Lewis. They would not be wrong. Our vision of this period for want of more precise data is essentially a reconstruction on the basis of our vision of the present world. It isn't improbable that the civilization was much more advanced in that period. So I shall limit myself to the most commonly held views of that time.

- **Social love of interest**: in the agriculturist-breeding era, marriages are arranged by the family. They are able, in this way, to seal unions of families or to recover much-envied lands from neighbors. This also explains the use of primogeniture to prevent land from being parceled out. Obviously this kind of love can also include physical and sexual love.

- **Free love** or **pure love**: the industry-commerce era sees the arrival of new forms of love that could be described as free love. So we ourselves choose our partner out of love. And when love vanishes, we divorce. This type of love often includes physical and sexual love and at times social love of interest as well. During certain periods, such as 1968 and the hippie era, a frenzied version of this kind of love was often visible.

- **Super Love**: a future evolution will see the coming of what Alvin Toffler calls 'Super Love' in which partners, besides love, look also for other forms of almost professional respect. Couples then spend more and more time at home (teleworking, micro business, etc.). People want to count on a truly trustworthy partner (in the business sense) to whom they can turn for advice. Intellectual respect and mutual esteem for each one's skills are fundamental. This type of love can include physical and sexual love, social love of interest and it often incorporates pure love as well.

- **Hyper Love**: in the creation-communication era, each one seeks to explore and work for the blossoming of his own uniqueness. So one looks for a true life-partner in the wider sense of the term, a person capable of pursuing his/her own development, both personal and spiritual. Love moves further and further away from conventional social patterns (marriage, divorce) and we see the emergence of new kinds of couples – for instance couples of the same sex or from more and more blended families that demand official recognition and their right to exist. This last type of love can obviously include all the preceding types but not always.

After genetic partners, social partners, romantic partners and business partners, we see now the emergence of spiritual partners! Evidently, in each era, large numbers of people do not attain the type of love most suitable for that period and remain at a form that is less evolved.

We also see differences appear within the life of the same couple. So you can have one partner criticizing the other for not giving him the right type of love: the partner thinks only of 'freeing his genetic potential' (to be read as 'my partner thinks only of shagging') or 'my partner isn't 'sufficiently romantic' (to be read as 'he or she thinks only about my money') or my partner is 'not sufficiently spiritual' (to be read as 'he or she is unbearably banal'), etc.

So, the solutions? Obviously to cultivate a more fractal vision of a couple's relationship! For many, this means having successive relationships in accordance with one's spiritual growth. Or having multiple relationships with different partners, in which each knows what type of love the other one brings (or does not) and what type of love he gives to the other.

What would be the relationship of a perfect fractal couple? Each one in the couple and the couple as an entity in itself, evolves in harmony through different types of love by knowing how to integrate them in a fractal way. So, I know how to be sexually aroused at certain moments and to celebrate romantically the life of a couple at others. I trust the expert counsel of my partner and together we evolve spiritually respecting each other's uniqueness towards a more integral and fractal relationship!

A new world culture?

If the question of living a couple's life is complex, the question of living in a group of seven billion people is equally complex, for sure! Until a few decades or centuries ago, men and women of different cultures met very little, after all. Only a few explorers were really confronted with cultural differences. We have already touched on this point a few times in this book: today we have the cultures of the world at our threshold at a mere click and human beings belonging to different cultures are led to meet one another or to have exchanges in the real or the digital world.

A fractal world culture

Remember what we saw in the first part of this book: 50,000 flights take off every day in the world. US$3200 billion a day change hands at the speed of light. 2500 satellites are circling the earth. Over five billion people possess a mobile phone and over two billion have access to the Internet. The majority of the seven billion human beings is directly or indirectly affected by a global worldwide activity. Even the significant part of humanity that has no electricity or is not yet connected still, remains involved in this globalized world most of the time, either indirectly or directly. The price of cereals produced by the small farmer in a developing country is probably determined at the Chicago stock exchange.

> I remember meeting in Bangalore the niece of a very close Indian friend. She had emigrated to the USA over ten years ago to pursue brilliant studies. After finishing, she started working in the Silicon Valley in California where she met her husband, also an Indian. two years ago they decided to return to India. Today she holds a highly important post in AOL in Bangalore. After her initial schooling in the USA, their little girl discovered India at ten. Our discussions dealt as much with Anglo-Saxon methods of management as with the different forms of Indian spirituality.

We see increasingly in certain countries people who had emigrated – often to the USA or sometimes to Europe, Canada or Australia to pursue their higher studies –, return to their country of birth since it offers them attractive advantages for coming back home and they are able to blossom at both a personal and a professional level.

Although migrations started from the very beginning of the human adventure, never have humans had such an interactive cultural relationship. Today millions of people have passports of at least two countries. Some of these people live between their country of adoption and their country of origin where they still have family and an increasingly professional activity or some business as well. Their children go to school in their country of adoption. Forty million Americans claim to be of another nationality.

The first emigrants, on leaving their country of origin, normally used to cut off all links with it forever. Returning home was far too expensive. News trickled in through the post once or several times a year. Today's emigrants can be in touch with their family and their country of origin via Internet any time. They speak and see each other regularly on Skype. On TV they follow the channels of their country via cable or satellite. They also take advantage of low-cost flights to travel home regularly.

So we have at once a global cosmopolitan culture and a world that is getting culturally and geographically more and more fractal. The culture of these new cosmopolitans mirrors, in an increasingly fractal way, the ethnic areas of a city. As Amin Maalouf explains, identities are overlapping, they are becoming multiple, they are becoming fractal.

People are meeting one another more and more, regardless of distance or culture. As a result, tourism is the biggest industry in the world in terms of value and represents over ten percent of the world GDP!

With the emergence of this new cosmopolitan world culture made up of both unity and diversity, we see a simultaneous emergence of a certain closing in on oneself and a rejection of the other, especially among the casualties of this globalization. The poorest are often its first victims. Forty percent of the planet's inhabitants earn less than US$2 a day to survive. Some of them, plunged into the daily struggle to meet their basic needs in order to survive, are going into a complete 'empathetic regression'. Quite understandably so, since only their own survival and that of their loved ones matters and the 'other' becomes increasingly a foreigner, why, very often even an enemy, the cause of his sufferings.

Both of these diametrically opposite cultural developments, one towards more empathy and unity in diversity, the other towards a closing in on oneself, racism and xenophobia, are one of the signs of the evolution of this 'human' system towards a turbulent and chaotic phase. And as we saw in the second part, the only outcome possible is either a breakdown of the human collectivity and an entry into a new age of darkness, or else the emergence of a new way of living together, a new era for humanity, more complex and more human!

We have passed from a binary or bipolar, North/South, East/West, developed/underdeveloped world to a multipolar one. Not very long ago, one or two 'empires' controlled most of the planet by means of their military and financial power. Today their power has become divided and fragmented. Power is shared by states, by NGOs, by mafia-controlled organizations, by multinationals, by religious powers (which formerly were always aligned with an empire), etc.

For many years I have been training French and European teams to work efficiently with Easterners. I often ask participants about the probability twenty years ago for a small town or large town entrepreneur from France to work on a daily basis, often far away and at times in the same office, with a Chinese or an Indian. It was almost non-existent. Internet did not exist then and even the few faxes sent did not match up in any way with a day at work today with its continual exchange of mails, telephone conversations, video-conferences and 'chat'. In certain sectors, it is almost impossible today not to have colleagues from across the world. We constantly need to remind ourselves that the world has shrunk! Conflicts no doubt, but also friendships between colleagues have become globalized.

The frontiers have come closer. The 'other', the 'foreigner' has become our neighbor, our colleague. And if new exacerbated forms of this closing in on oneself are visible – expressions of racism and xenophobia –, we also see developing across continents new friendly bonds or at least mutually respectful relations.

And this is nothing compared with the virtual world! One can have dozens, hundreds or thousands of friends in cyberspace. Relations of friendship have themselves changed. The virtual connections influence the way we experience strong emotional moments of our life, be they happy or sad. How many of us, including myself, learnt about the illness or the passing of a dear one on Facebook? The impact of the tsunami in Japan and the accident in the nuclear plant of Fukushima in 2011 triggered very strong emotions and movements of solidarity far beyond the countries affected. The awareness of the other has been globalized. Jeremy Rifkin speaks of the emergence of new forms of empathy. Empathy for one's dear ones and for one's clan developed first into empathy for one's country and now into trans-national empathy.

The world according to Huntington... and the world we want to build!

A few years ago, Samuel Huntington wrote a highly successful book *The Clash of Civilizations*. This success redoubled post-9/11 (2001) by popularizing the presumed conflict between the Muslim and the Western world.

Huntington explains in his book that the world is divided into major distinctive civilizations and some of them think it is their vocation to fight with each other. So he gives us a map of these civilizations:

The world according to Samuel Huntington

I think this well-demarcated world with clearly defined boundaries no longer exists. This map has become an illusion and is but an after-image of a world that is no more. Today, the other, the foreigner, can be one's neighbor or one's colleague at work. I have more in common with my friend Jawhara from Cairo, with my friend Kai from China, my friend Danya from New York and with so many others geographically far removed from me than I have with some of my neighbors.

Everywhere in the real world, different communities are developing locally and perhaps even more locally in the virtual one. I think the civilizational map today looks more like this fractal image:

The world according to Bruno Marion

I believe that it is no more time for war *between* civilizations but the time for war *in favor of* civilization.

Let Huntington be unhappy but it is not a time for the clash of civilizations but the time of clash *for* a civilization.

The evolution of writing

Our cultures and modes of thinking are very much linked to the way we write. And if we attentively observe certain developments of writing, we shall realize that even in writing, the linear boundaries are blurring and giving birth to new ways of writing and thus, in the long run, to new ways of thinking.

There are in the world two ways of writing: analytical writing with an alphabet (all Western scripts) and analog, visual writing (Chinese being the most widespread).

Let us focus on the principal differences between these two types of writing.

Analytic writing

- It uses an alphabet.
- It is conceptual and logical.
- What is important is the symbol formed by the letters.
- If there is a typing mistake, it does not usually change the meaning.
- The meaning of a word varies little with regard to context.
- One reads mostly from left to right (there are exceptions that can be explained) which favors the use of the left brain.
- We derive sense in a conceptual manner from signs (letters) which do not have an intrinsic meaning.

Following the writing it uses, Western thought is conceptual, logical and not too bothered about detail.

Try to read the following text:

> Aoccdrnig to a rscheearch at an Elingsh uinervtisy, it deosn't mttaer in waht oredr the ltteers in a wrod are, the olny iprmoetnt tihng is taht the frist and lsat ltteer is at the rghit pclae. The rset can be a toatl mses and you can sitll raed it wouthit porbelm. Tihs is bcuseae we do not raed ervey lteter by itslef but the wrod as a wlohe.

In spite of the mistakes, most people catch perfectly the meaning of the text!

Another example? What can you read inside the triangle below?

Have you read correctly? Are you sure? Check the footnote.[6]

---

[6] It is written in the triangle: 'I love Paris in the the springtime'. We have the word THE twice. Had you noticed it? Western writing does not favor this sensibility to detail and only fifteen percent of readers notice the second THE.

Analog writing (Chinese)

- It is contextual.
- It is based on an imaged reality, not on a symbol.
- The detail is important. An error in the 'drawing' can make it illegible or completely change the meaning.
- The context is essential. The same ideogram will completely change meaning in relation with the ideograms that surround it.
- You read from right to left which favours the use of the right brain (there are some exceptions that can be explained).
- We derive sense by drawing and recounting stories.

Like its writing, Chinese thought is contextual and very sensitive to detail.

These two types of writing, linked to two types of thinking, can they meet? Will we see some forms of writing appear that get fractalized with visual aspects in conceptual scripts like the Latin alphabet? And inversely, will we see conceptual and logical aspects in alphabets that are typically visual and contextual like the Chinese? Will this contribute to creating a new form of more fractal thinking?

Indeed, such phenomena are already happening!

Japan today possesses two ways of writing. The first uses Chinese ideograms, the kanji, with the accompanying influences on thinking as described above. The second way uses the two-syllabled alphabet, *hiragana* and *katakana*. This way of writing leads to a more conceptual thinking and is closer to the Western mode of thinking linked with the analytical writing. This may be what explains the special place Japan occupies in Asia and the world.

The example of Korean is perhaps even more interesting. First, Korean is probably among the last alphabets invented in the 15th century. Prior to this, Chinese ideograms were used. So Hangul, the Korean alphabet, can be considered to be recent at the scale of our history. It could also be a precursor. If Korean is typically phonetic and so conceptual and logical, it takes on a very visual aspect. Looking at a Korean billboard, an uninitiated tourist might believe it is Chinese!

But here's more. When King Sejong invented the Hangul alphabet, he based himself on the forms of the organs (mouth, tongue) that produce the corresponding sounds in order to draw the different letters of the alphabet.

So to an initiated person, Korean writing resembles analog visual writing, like the Chinese, but is, in fact, an analytic conceptual writing with an alphabet which is based on the visual!

I notice then that even in writing, the clear boundaries are getting blurred to make way for new forms of writing. So we see visual and contextual elements appear in analytic writing:

- The appearance of smileys in mails, in SMS, in instant messaging, etc.

- The contextual writing of SMS with certain phones that have a software for intuitive writing.

- Look at the impossibility of understanding certain SMS out of context "AAR8, my Ps wr ☺ - they sd ICBW, & tht they wr ha-p 4 the pc&qt..." For the more aged amongst us, it means: "At any rate, my parents were happy - they said it could be worse, and that they were happy with the peace and quiet.".

We can also observe the appearance of more analytic forms of writing with the Chinese. If you receive the following SMS from a Chinese person, think well before answering!

51095

It means (in fact it sounds like when you read it in Cantonese):

我要你嫁我

Which means in English: "I would like you to marry me"!

So we observe that a new form of fractal writing, both visual-contextual and logical-conceptual is emerging. It is for us to learn to identify it and above all to learn to utilize it to make our communication richer. It is also in this way that we shall work for the emergence of a new way of thinking... and a new form of fractal consciousness!

A more fractal civilization and humanity

Another way of observing the development of cultures is to observe Man's activities over the centuries. Among other things, the evolution of humanity has gone through many changes in life-styles and techniques. We can distinguish four eras: hunter-gathering, agriculturist-breeding, industry-commerce and the present era that is rising of creation-communication.

The transition towards the creation-communication society is very different from the preceding transitions. This because of two main characteristics: speed and its fractal aspect which we have alluded to. It is important to remember this when we look at the way principal human activities have changed.

First of all, speed. The preceding transitions took place over several thousand or several hundred years whereas the present transition is taking place in merely a few decades –, almost within a generation! And for the first time in our history, millions or billions, of people are going to live through a change of reference points, values, and modes of functioning in the course of their lives.

The other major difference from the preceding transitions is that this time the transition appears to be more fractal. The preceding transitions were in fact very linear or binary. Even if, and perhaps because of this, they unfolded over very long periods, the new era was seen to replace the previous one almost completely. Thus, the farmers-breeders almost completely eliminated the hunters-gatherers. In the same way, the farmers-breeders were almost entirely industrialized and financialized. Less than three percent of the population in France today participates in an activity of animal husbandry or agriculture.

The transition towards the creation-communication society, precisely because it is so fast compared to previous ones, will allow and necessitate the cohabitation of hunters-gatherers and non-industrial agriculturists-breeders. Needless to say we shall continue to cherish several positive aspects acquired during the industry-commerce era, such as the advances in health and individual liberties, for instance.

We will then see the appearance of a humanity like a fractal image in which each person can find his or her place. And obviously, as in a fractal image, each succeeding era will assimilate and carry forward some aspects of the preceding eras.

- **The hunters-gatherers**: the creation-communication society will help them to spread their culture, traditions and knowhow. While talking with ethnologists of the Australian aborigines, for instance, I was surprised to learn how these populations have already adopted the new tools of communication and many among them have joined 'the network'. Some of them even affirm that they find it quite 'natural'. And today's shamans have no hesitation in boarding a plane to go and meet their fellow-members in another country or in another culture, or simply out of a need for survival from the ongoing destruction of their habitat. Edgar Morin reminds us in *La Voie*, that video has made it possible for young natives to preserve their knowledge and their distinctive traditions.

- **The farmers-breeders**: we are going to see both in the developing and the developed countries a more food-growing, environment-friendly and consumer-friendly agriculture reappear. In every country, farmers will assimilate the best elements of the industry-commerce era (who wants to do away with the cold-room?) and the creation-communication era. I always encourage my farmer friends in Ardèche to go in for more integration of production; I urge them not merely to produce raw material but also finished products with it. For instance, not just produce milk but make cheese as well. Similarly, I advise them to join farmers' market through which they can have direct contact with the customer. Thus, their Dutch tourist customer is able to keep ordering products from them on the Internet all through the year and in this way fulfil to some extent his longing for the Ardèche countryside.

- **Industry-commerce**: societies that are at present anchored in the industry-commerce era, the enterprises, have already to a great extent integrated and assimilated the technologies of the creation-communication era. This basically explains the tremendous gains in productivity made by them in these last years. The main challenge for persons and organizations that are primarily industry-commerce oriented is to find a harmony with the other hunter-gatherer and ariculturist-breeding eras and with nature. They will have to evolve from a predatory culture towards a culture of development that is more respectful and harmonious. We shall talk about this most significant aspect in the rest of the book.

- **The members of the creation-communication society** will be able to incorporate into their lives more naturally and more easily all the preceding eras. From a cyclic vision one can imagine an immensely successful businessman sell his firm in order to buy a vineyard and so return to the activity of a farmer when he is not gathering mushrooms or hunting (in Appleton WI?) like a hunter-gatherer. From a more fractal vision of evolution, one can see the simultaneous appearance of the nearly vanished ancestral practices along with very current or even futuristic ones. Thus one relearns to peel one's vegetables instead of buying frozen or canned stuff and, at the same time, one takes a cooking or management course on the Internet. One relearns to cultivate one's organic kitchen garden whereas elsewhere we handle the main part of our activities online on a tablet or smartphone. We travel by bullet train... and bicycle. We rediscover the lost pleasure of walking and we drive a hybrid car. We rediscover the pleasure of reading old books and at the same watch an online conference live on our PC. We relearn to chop wood to heat the house in addition to the already installed solar heating with its high-tech controls, etc.

A new fractal ethic

Ethics are a very important aspect of cultures and they strongly influence our way of living together. Every culture has its own ethic and today these ethics are clashing increasingly in a turbulent and chaotic manner.

Western ethics is essentially based on the relation to good and evil which leads us straight to guilt. It is man who chooses good and evil. The free will that is given to him comes with the responsibility of making the right choice. On the other hand, if he makes the wrong choice, that is if he is guilty, he will be judged by God or His representatives, ultimately condemned and stripped of his freedom.

Western ethics is absolute and the opinion of others does not count. If you know that you act rightly, you needn't bother about what people say. At their negative extreme, Western ethics sows the seeds of egoism and individualism.

On the contrary, Eastern ethics is about saving face: what do others think of my actions? Good or bad, being very relative and complementary, are born from each other and complete each other harmoniously. I also know what is appropriate for me to do by observing and respecting the rules of my group. What I do should be acceptable to it. If it is not acceptable, then I lose face. In a situation where there is a serious loss of face, I am not stripped of my freedom; on the contrary, I get back my freedom and I am banned, excluded from the group. At its negative extreme, Eastern ethics, especially Confucian, sows the seeds for a collectivism that crushes the individual.

Today the dual Western vision of good and evil has reached its limits in a world that has grown complex and is constantly changing ever faster. Likewise, the absolute priority given to face and group in Asia has reached its limits in a world that has grown at once globalized and is moving towards the universal. The human collective, in order to succeed or simply to survive in a complex chaotic world, has an absolute need to ensure that every individual can fully express his otherness and uniqueness. In a chaotic world, diversity is no more a choice but the very basis of survival. Likewise, in a chaotic mode, unity is no more a choice but a necessity of survival. Unity and diversity must therefore complement each other harmoniously.

The collectivity and the individual, the permanent and the transient come together and complete each other in a sublime poetic fractal image.

The question is no longer guilt or innocence with regard to a law that is presumed universal. The question is no longer loss of or saving face with regard to the group. The question is about conscience. Are my choices in life, my daily acts, mere automatisms, fruits of conditioning; do they follow a law that is presumed to be universal or the rules of my group? Or are they made 'in awareness' and therefore perfectly in tune with my values and those of my group and with the complexity of the moment? This 'awareness' and the need to act 'in awareness' is found at the root of all great religions or philosophies. It is only men and time that have replaced them with simplified versions such as guilt and saving face. It is now indispensable to return to the roots and adapt them to the complexity of our world in metamorphosis.

CHAOS, A USERS GUIDE

In this fast-changing world, the breakthrough, the transformation, is that the individual, the 'I', in his freed otherness, in his multiple identities, become an indispensable member of the collectivity, the 'we' that no more emerges only at the level of a family, a group or a nation but at the level of the human species which is both diverse and unique.

The emergence of a new collective fractal consciousness: it is already there!

The new collective consciousness will be fractal. And this new global consciousness is already dawning upon earth! Obviously if you remain in the linear vision you won't see it. By linear vision I mean a vision in which we project existing tendencies and base ourselves on current models in order to understand and make projections. On the other hand, with a fractal vision, you can see this new form of collective consciousness emerging. By fractal vision, I understand the capacity to identify the patterns of a fractal image within the apparent chaos created by these multiple overlapping and interconnected new frontiers. That is to say, I am able to identify among the weak signals those that constitute real new triggers of emergence!

A few examples:

- Never in the history of humanity have so many people across the world marched against a war, the second war in the Gulf.

If you look at this with your linear-binary vision, you will only see setbacks in their endeavor to stop this war that eventually did break out. With a fractal vision, you will see that in addition to the record size of these protests, it is no longer a question of a simple binary confrontation between countries for or against the war, but that even larger protests happened in those very countries that were part of the 'coalition' that was supporting the war. The protest by one and a half million people in London is then not only the most important of all the protests but also the most important in the country's entire history! You will thus see the beginning of the emergence of this new fractal global consciousness!

- Never had there been such a volume of donations following a natural disaster, the Tsunami of December 2004.

With a linear-binary vision, you will only see an upsurge of generosity proportionate to the gravity of the catastrophe and the difficulties faced in the utilization or non-utilization of these donations. With a fractal vision, you will see another precursor of the emergence of this new global consciousness: people who had never given before, contributed in this upsurge of worldwide generosity, even in countries more accustomed to receiving global aid than giving. It – the hyper media coverage of the event, is not the only explanation for this incredible inflow of aid. It is the emergence of the global consciousness that is struggling to respond, on a planetary scale, to problems that are themselves of a planetary scale: climate change, pollution, new pandemics, etc.

- The rapid development of microcredit is another example. We have moved from a system where large lenders lend to large borrowers or to borrowers who are in any case solvent, to a system where each is *both* a borrower and a lender, to a system that also includes the less solvent.

With a linear-binary vision, you will only see an extension of the capitalistic, financier world to the poorest. With a fractal vision, you will see the emergence of a new form of economic and social organization that assimilates those who were left out until now by the prevalent system. You will see a new proof of the emergence of the fractal global consciousness.

- Couchsurfing is an international non-profit association that links up travelers with local hosts who offer free hospitality. Over one million 'couch surfers' have already made use of this in the world. Since its creation in 2003, its members have reported almost five million experiences that were considered 99.7 percent positive. And according to its members, 2.9 million friendships were born, of which 100,000 turned out to be very close! Couchsurfing promotes the idea that we are all members of a world community.

So, with a linear-binary vision, you will only see in each of these individual actions, in each NGO, in each humanitarian enterprise, or in each emergence of an Internet social network, merely isolated projects that cannot simply be generalized or replicated on a larger scale and which will, therefore, never attain that critical mass capable of solving problems on a planetary scale. With a fractal vision you will see, on the contrary, the emergence of a new global consciousness. You know that the critical size has no meaning in a chaotic world. You will see the seed crystals of solutions to planetary scale problems, the potential butterfly effects.

The more alert among us believe they are seeing weak signals and base their forecasts on them. But these examples are not the weak signals of a linear universe. They are strong signals of a chaotic and fractal universe.

They do not announce new changes, they are proofs of a whole new organization that is emerging. It is for us to see and learn to be part of this new emergence. If we observe these new signs, we can then help take part in and facilitate this emergence. On the contrary, if we miss this chance, we shall only aggravate the suffering and the catastrophes.

The emergence of a new global consciousness is at once necessary and inevitable. It will happen sooner or later but we have the collective choice to make it happen now... or later. In peace for the well-being of the largest number... or in pain and suffering. It is a historic individual and collective choice. Such an occasion has never come before in our history!

Beyond the real

> In 2004, David Storey entered the Guinness records at the age of 22 for having bought 'the most expensive virtual object', namely a virtual island in the online Project Entropia for US$26,500. David isn't out of his head, he wanted to make money. So today he looks after his island that he has transformed into a hunting reserve (virtual, don't forget) and he earns money from hunting rights that he sells to hunters (also virtual) who visit his island. He thus earns more than US$100,000 a year, very real dollars these!

Another frontier that is becoming less and less binary is the one between the real and the virtual. Never have the real and the virtual overlapped so much, making their boundaries more and more blurred. For example we used to say, "I'm going on the Net". That was our linear vision: I was either online or offline. For the youth of today, the expression 'I'm going on the Net' doesn't mean anything or at most it amuses them. The Internet has become embedded in life. Real life and virtual life are no longer divided by a clear, distinct frontier. The real world spills over into the virtual and vice versa. So with geo-localization software we can finally 'see' through walls: we can, in fact, know whether our friends are inside the café we are going past, so that we can go in and meet them if we wish or avoid them if we don't. The 'augmented reality' allows us, thanks to our mobile phones or some special lenses, to retrieve more information than our eyes can provide. Thus the visiting hours of a museum we are passing, get automatically displayed on the screen, the apartments on sale on the street we are visiting are listed with their prices and even the contact details of the real-estate agency!

We now observe with our fractal vision that the real and the virtual are not on two separate planes anymore. The virtual overlaps on to the real and vice versa. And if the real overlaps on to the virtual, the virtual overlaps as much on to the real: in order to have news of our neighbor, it is easier to type his name on Google than to go and knock on his door! Once again, the real is in the virtual and the virtual is in the real, both joined as in a fractal image.

One day when I asked a child who had come to visit me in my house in Ardèche why he wasn't going out to play and not making the best of nature, he replied: "But all the electronic games are inside, not outside the house!" QED! So to replace this very binary frontier between the natural and the artificial, we might imagine some video games that help us discover nature, the principles of life and of ecosystems. But especially to help children remain in contact with 'real' nature, which will never be replaced by virtual worlds, couldn't we create experiences, tracking-games, adventures in nature with the reality highlighted on their mobile phones or their gaming consoles? Today over fifty percent live in urban milieus and increasing numbers of children are no longer exposed to nature. It is essential for our little city-dwellers, for their equilibrium, why even for their survival and that of our planet, to retrace the road back to nature. And this road cannot simply be 'a return to nature'. It must base itself on the culture of the youngsters today, not on the glorified memories of our romantic past.

Living together, the analogy with life

To conclude this part of the evolution of our relationships with others and with other cultures, we can take nature once again for inspiration. If the analogies of the linear world were almost all issued from mechanics and physics, the analogies to understand and adapt to a turbulent and chaotic world must take inspiration from life and from biology. We shall have the chance to come back to this very soon in the chapter on organizations.

Life has been able to adapt for millenniums in order to survive, grow and evolve in environments that are naturally turbulent and chaotic. Let us then observe the principal characteristics of each cell that has made such an achievement possible.

- **A higher goal**: a cell agrees first to work for the well-being and survival of the body as a whole; it looks after its own interests only subsequently. The cell is ready to sacrifice itself and die in order to protect and ensure the growth of the whole. Each cell in our body, therefore, lives but a fraction of the time of our entire life. Thus egoism is not a viable alternative.

- **Exchange**: a cell is always in contact and communication with other cells. Messenger molecules wander around the whole body in order to keep track of what is going on even in its remotest part. The absence of exchange and communication, therefore, is not a viable alternative.

- **Consciousness**: a cell is conscious of each moment. It is capable of adapting to any change of circumstances, however sudden, and to respond to it in an adequate manner. Being shut up in unchanging habits is then not a viable alternative.

- **Otherness**: a cell recognizes and accepts the importance of all the other types of cells. Every bodily function is important and inter-dependent. Going it alone is thus not a viable alternative.

- **Creativity**: even if each cell has a well-defined role, different roles combine in a creative manner. Thus we are able to digest food we have eaten for the first time in our life, we are able to dance to a dance we are not familiar with and we are able to get ideas never thought before. Routine and absence of creativity are, then, not viable alternatives.

- **Being**: a cell knows how to simply be. It knows how to respect the cycle of activity and rest. Without sleep, the cell and the body would die. The cell knows how to respect silence. Rest and silence are an indispensable part of life. Relentless activity, physical or mental, is not, therefore, a viable alternative.

- **Efficiency**: a cell functions with the minimum use of energy. It also stocks a very small quantity of it, equal to three seconds of supply. It trusts the whole completely to provide it with what is required. An excessive consumption of food, water, energy is not then a viable alternative.

- **Links**: a cell knows, beyond differences and distinctive natures, that it shares the same DNA as its peers. Liver cells are different from the heart cells. The cells of the skin are different from those in the brain. However, they all know that they share the same identity that transcends them. Separating oneself from the community is thus not a viable alternative.

- **Giving**: the essential activity of the cell is to give, which fosters the existence of other cells and the soundness of the whole. There is a total commitment to giving which constitutes one half of the natural cycle; the other half is receiving. So, hoarding and stinginess are not viable alternatives.

- **Immortality**: the cell reproduces itself in order to transmit its knowledge, its experience and its talents. It does not hold back anything for itself and hands over everything to its descendants. This is how it achieves a kind of immortality. The conflict of generations, then, is not a viable alternative.

Let us ask ourselves if we can be like our cells, not at the scale of the cell in the body but at the scale of humans as part of humanity. In this way we can naturally and instinctively find the means not only to survive but more importantly to live and to blossom individually and collectively at the scale of humanity. We will then be ready for the breakthrough described by the theories of chaos in the second part of this book. We will thus be capable of realizing our own metamorphosis and the metamorphosis of humanity towards a more complex and a more harmonious system in which each person finds their place in a natural and organic way.

Let us see which institutional tools, which systems of education and which forms of governance we can use to help us.

The Collective: a more fractal society, institutions, learning and organizations? (The true)

We have seen how the individual human being could evolve in a turbulent, chaotic world. We have also observed how the relationship of couples could evolve as well as our relationship with others and with our cultures. Now let us focus on how our institutions, our modes of consumption and our schools can evolve in order to adapt to this fast-changing world. We shall then see how to ensure the survival and the growth of organizations and companies.

Towards a more just, more efficient, more fractal democracy?

What process of common life, of collective decision-making, could we set in place to make democracy operational in a world that has become turbulent and chaotic? This question is most urgent – we cannot continue to live any longer under the illusion of linear democracy in a world that has become chaotic and fractal. Our democratic organization must be adapted to a world that has changed! Only new processes of Collective Intelligence can respond to these new needs for a harmonious and efficient functioning of the 'City'.

Our democratic vision is essentially binary today:
-   Two political parties in general (or reduced to two in the second round of election).
-   The winning party in the election gets all the powers for a given period.

In this linear-visioned democracy, we elect the so-called more competent ones among the citizens so that they can govern us in an enlightened and efficient way. This implies that they are the most competent for the entire duration of their mandate and for all the functions for which they were elected. This democratic organization was no doubt the best (or "the worst system of government, with the exception of all the others that have been tried out in history" according to Churchill). That is indeed true. It is perfectly adapted to systems where few people have the necessary knowledge (the more educated in a society, the elite, objectively speaking) and it functions well when the phenomena are less complex and at a scale of time that is much slower.

In this linear, binary vision, we are supposed to elect those we consider most capable of taking the right decisions in the common interest, the most competent among citizens so that they can govern us in an enlightened, efficient way. And this for a period of four to five years. Now who can believe today that in this chaotic world a person can have the capacities to grasp the existing complexity and take the right decisions on very diverse subjects that are getting ever more complex? And this for a duration of several years? Who can still believe that if our leaders do not have the necessary abilities that doesn't really matter; they can always surround themselves with good advisors or the right experts? Experts who are increasingly shut up in the ivory tower of their subject of specialization whereas the analysis of a complex world requires, on the contrary, an increasingly transversal vision. Today information is accessible to all and fragmented as well: your next door neighbor probably knows more about the future of bees than your elected Member of Parliament!

These days, democracy is no longer 'the best system for want of another'. It is indispensable to find better ones. There have been some endeavors and experiments and this must continue by trying out new things, changing old ways and exploring new paths. Participatory democracy is certainly one of the most promising endeavors among these.

I think there must be two lines of thinking for a democratic functioning adapted to an increasingly complex and fractal world:

- **'Multi-layered' decision-systems** going from the local to global. It is evident that complex and universal problems like global warming, financial crisis, etc. can no longer be resolved at the local or even the national level. It is only at the international or supra-national level that they can be dealt with. Sooner or later, universal forms of governance will become indispensable. Likewise, it seems quite insane to resolve local problems at the national or international level.

Seen from this perspective, France with its 37,000 communes (half the number of the European Union total) which are often criticized, and the European experiment in general, which is also often scoffed at, are undoubtedly examples to be spread.

- **Participatory democracy-type decision-making systems**. In such a democratic system, we could, for instance, think of creating bodies composed of well-known specialists, elected representatives, officers nominated by a competent administration, and citizens chosen randomly. We could constitute panels of concerned partners (clients, suppliers, regulators, users, elected representatives, etc.) who would take the decisions. The main idea is to give such bodies or panels the necessary time and means to acquaint themselves with the subject as well as they can, and to decide on the process of governance that would allow the body to take the best decisions. Such systems are in no way utopian. They exist and have amply proved how effective their functioning can be.

We could then evolve towards democratic systems that are more in tune with our ever more complex and fast-changing world. A system of democracy that is more integral, more fractal.

A digression: are polls/surveys to be believed?

Some people affirm unhesitatingly today that we are governed by polls. But are these polls truly able to foresee the results of elections? Can they really tell us what a given population thinks? Even though pollsters themselves, as well as journalists at times, remind us that polls are but a snapshot, a reflection, they are nevertheless used by political analysts and everyone as information for the impending results of the elections or on the assumed opinion of the population.

So two questions come up: do polls really give us accurate information on the results of elections? and are they really a reflection, a snapshot of public opinion? The answer to both these questions is negative.

Pollsters themselves do not claim any more that polls are tools for forecasting.

Moreover, even if polls can inform us about the opinions of the persons polled and their evolution in time, they in no way reflect a faithful image, a snapshot of public opinion (if at all that exists). The reason is straightforward: polls are essentially based on linear and/or temporal projections:

- If so many among the cross-section of people polled behave in this way, then x percent of the population will behave the same way.

- If the people polled provided us in the past with certain information on the overall population, we can advance the same hypothesis, why, we can even make the desirable corrections in the current results, keeping the past in mind.

Well, all this cannot hold any longer and rightly so! As we have begun to observe, the world is no longer linear, it has become chaotic, it has become fractal. And here too, we have several examples:

- The choice itself of the sample of those polled raises a problem. How do you project results that were obtained from a sample of people as they were got in the past, when twenty percent of people do not have a landline (those polled are even today often interviewed over their landline), especially among younger voters?

- More important still, we are seeing the emergence of what we might compare to the loops of positive feedback that we described in the second part of this book: those polled choose to answer in conformity with their desire to manipulate the result of the poll.

- And let us not forget the phenomenon of the influence of the observer on the thing observed. So it is about the choice of pollsters to conduct polls on possible future scenarios of the second round in presidential election with candidates that should not have gone beyond the first round as per their own polls!

However, these polls should not be taken to be pointless. It is the way they are used that is excessive.

Today, in a non-linear world that has become fractal, these polls are probably more relevant than ever. But the probabilities and statistics must now be in consonance with the theory of chaos. So, polls should highlight two things that are essential in rightly observing and understanding a fractal world:

152

- Polls allow us to follow the changes in time.

What are the answers given to the same questions by a sampling of people living in different periods?

- Polls are an invaluable tool in providing us with different possible scenarios.

Rather than foresee one and only one possible future reality, namely the most probable, polls allow us to work on different possible outcomes.

In a linear world, it is true, we can make projections, but in a fractal world, we can paint scenarios, we can see different possible paths. Seeing these scenarios is like seeing fractal images emerge from what seems to be chaos; it is seeing order in disorder.

It would be a pity to throw the baby out with the bathwater! We need more than ever analytic and projection tools. We need to unify the science of probability with the science of chaos in our methods of polling, as is happening already in the field of meteorology and finance, for example.

Let us learn how to use polls for what they can bring us, and a little less for our bar-room discussions.

A more fractal production-consumption-elimination chain?

Even though we have seen that our activity must focus more and more on communication and creation, the production and consumption of material goods are not going to disappear. We must continue to eat, to dress and to move. The ecological stakes that we briefly mentioned in the first part urge us to study how a less binary, linear vision can be applied to this aspect of things. We shall see once again how a more fractal vision opens up new leads before us.

The life of products that we consume is much too linear at present:

Extraction of raw material → Production → Consumption → Elimination or stocking of waste at end of life

Linear product life: production – consumption - waste

This linear chain is responsible for the ecological catastrophes that erupt before us and alas, will continue to do so. If it has triggered an incredible development for an important part of the population (but not the whole), it cannot continue to function in a sustainable way on a planet where resources are not unlimited. I think it is only crazy people (and the economists) who believe that there can be an unlimited growth on a limited planet with naturally limited resources.

A less linear and more cyclic vision can make possible for a more sustainable development, that is, a development which will preserve the planet for future generations while guaranteeing the development of the present population. The most evident cyclical contribution in the life of products towards a more sustainable development is obviously recycling. Doing one's bit is the least we can expect from everyone, and sorting out one's waste and one's trashcan!

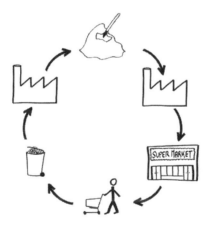

Cyclic product life: production – consumption - recycling

Recycling is a good start, but it won't suffice. All the products, in reality, are not totally recyclable on their expiry. And what happens at the different stages of production? What do we do with the intermediary waste that was useful in the different stages of manufacturing? It is good to recycle but if the production of what we buy has destroyed half the planet, it is not enough to preserve it!

We can go further even than the linear (extraction of raw materials, production, consumption, elimination) and even than the cyclic (recycling). We require a more global vision, a vision more integral and more fractal in which the life of a product is both linear *and* cyclic. Each stage of production, consumption and expiry is then a subject of reflection where the waste of one product becomes the raw material for another, like living organisms where the waste of one is the raw material of the other.

It is not just recycling at expiry but permanent recycling that needs to be done at every stage! This mode of production and life of products exists already and is called 'from cradle to cradle.' We are talking here of a real fractal image that assimilates and unifies at every level the conception, production and recycling of products – this is an ecological requirement of which the principle is zero percent pollution and one hundred percent recycling. Simply put, it means that a product which is manufactured must be able, once it has been recycled, to produce once again the same product, with just the addition of renewable energy coming into the cycle.

X

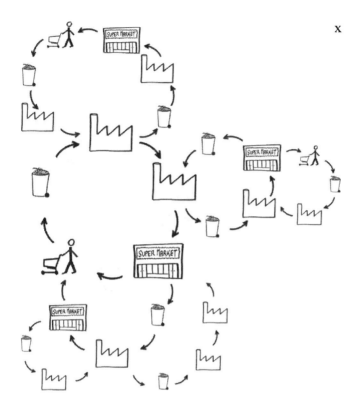

Fractal product life: production – consumption – recycling

Such a change in our ways of production and consumption is not a luxury but an inevitable change of strategy and it is hugely exciting for the survival of the planet, as well as for our survival!

Fractal energy networks

We saw in the first part that the present world depends mainly on fossil energy, petrol in particular. The energy angle is absolutely inescapable since our needs will probably continue to grow for two reasons. Unless there's a collapse, if the population keeps rising, the global needs in energy will also grow in a linear fashion. But in addition, the theories of chaos teach us that the more a system is complex, the more energy it needs. In fact, the more a system is complex and 'evolved', the more it is 'fragile'. The more a system is complex and evolved, the more energy it requires to maintain its existence. It will, therefore, require more energy, or a more efficient use of the available energy. Nature confirms it. An ant, in proportionate to its weight, requires less energy every day than a mammal does to ensure its survival. And as humanity will become more complex, the challenges of the energy sector will become pivotal.

The energy-transition is a key question for the future of humanity. In fact, it is indispensable that we start thinking about it right away. And it could become an exhilarating adventure: what would you say about living in a world free of pollution?

Jeremy Rifkin shows clearly in *The Empathic Civilization* and in *The Third Industrial Revolution* how we are going to pass from a mechanistic, hierarchical and centralized vision of energy to a fractal vision of a distributed electric grid in which every building is a mini electric power station connected to the grid.

Thus, in my house in Ardèche, we are connected to the electricity network and we produce photovoltaic as well as wind energy which is re-injected into the grid when we don't use it. In case of a problem on the grid (breakdown, storm), we can continue to run as an independent unit by consuming all the energy we produce by stocking it in batteries for the periods when there is no sun or wind. Our installation automatically reconnects with the grid as soon as the problem is solved. It is important to note that even though I do not refer here to one of the essential aspects of the energy-transition, namely the increase in energy efficiency (and therefore, a reduction in individual consumption), we have been able to reduce our consumption for lighting in the house by seven to eight, especially by using low-consumption lights, compact fluorescent lamp and specially LED bulbs. Thus in the end, we produce a little more electricity than we consume (counting both our houses in Ardèche and in Paris).

And it is in this way that we will be able to go from (almost) completely nuclear, (almost) completely petrol to smart grids that combine multiple energies in a fractal image, which will develop rapidly towards greater use of renewable non-carbonaceous energies.

Up till now we have been either consumer *or* producer. Now we are becoming more and more consumer *and* producer. We receive from the grid *and* we re-inject into the grid. The linear and pyramidal organization of the production and distribution of energy becomes a beautiful fractal image in which each one is both a producer *and* a consumer.

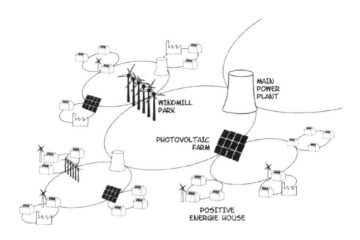

Fractal smart grid

A fractal galaxy of currencies

Along with fossil energy, finance itself, the other pillar on which the present world rests, is founded on the principle of rare currencies, that is on 'money'.

When I talk about currencies, I notice that it elicits a maximum of questions… and of opposition. It seems that for most people, telling them that their world is crumbling; (okay, why not) that the world of work will be revolutionized; (fine) that the systems of education will explode; (quite normal)… but that the present system of currencies will change; (no way, impossible!) Money thus is truly anchored at the center of our beliefs. It is, however, one of the examples, I feel, that is both most obvious and most pivotal in the evolution of our way of living together.

The present system rests on a few rare currencies, the most common being the Dollar, the Euro, the Yen, the Yuan, etc. In a linear vision, it is a limited number of currencies that allows us to evaluate, exchange and pass on wealth. In a linear vision, the question of the day is "Will the Euro replace the Dollar?" or "Will the Yuan, the Chinese currency, replace the others in ten to twenty years?" In a more fractal vision, the valuation, exchange and transfer of wealth, in the widest meaning of the term, will happen in various ways. For certain national and international exchanges, we might have certain rare currencies, why even one transnational currency composed of an international basket of currencies (the Dollar, Euro, Yuan, Real, Yen, etc.). And beside these 'classical' currencies, there would be a multitude of other currencies. We have observed for the last several years, with a recent acceleration, the development of thousands of so-called 'complementary' currencies. The next stage

– and the real revolution – will be with 'free' currencies, free systems of valuation, exchange and free transfer of wealth conceived by the communities that use them; these communities will adopt the notion and creation of currency in accordance with their own rules.

If you have enjoyed free software, you will adore free currencies. And if you don't believe in the future of free software and free currencies, get ready for some terrific surprises! What will follow rare currencies, the well-defined boundaries of a linear world, is a constellation, a fractal galaxy, from the most international currency to the most local or the most specialized ones.

The valuation, exchange and transfer of wealth (from one generation to the next, for example) have always been an important aspect of human relations. We may also compare it with the living, and observe that the exchange of wealth is at the heart of living organisms. It is therefore natural that a fast-changing world looks at this domain, as with issues of energy which are equally at the heart of life, and moves towards a model that is more adapted to a turbulent and chaotic world, a model more inspired by life than by the mechanical, a model that will necessarily be more fractal.

Education

Education is a fundamental challenge, both in terms of culture and as an institution. Along with increasingly evolved forms of education that are emerging in methods of learning, cooperation and development of the child, we also observe the re-emergence of hysterical forms of education in the old-fashioned mould. 'Tiger mom' and 'Tiger dad' would in this vision represent, through their caricatural authority, the future of education. We see once more the appearance of the 'turbulent' zone described in the evolution of chaotic systems in the world in the second part of the book. The system has come out of equilibrium and attained forms that are further and further from the old equilibrium. And the methods of the old world are being pushed to a level that seems hysterical and parodic. So for some, the future of education is a return to the multiplication table and the hit on the knuckles. When will we start justifying the dunce's cap? I think we are seeing here the signs of a regression or breakdown of a system of the past, a system that has become obsolete. Will we be capable of making a new breakthrough and inventing new forms of education adapted to a new civilization?

We shall see here how we can have a less linear approach to education, an approach that is more fractal and responds to the challenges of a turbulent and chaotic world. We shall focus especially on the different methods of education, on time management and on the organization of space.

Conceptual Western education or practical Eastern learning: towards a fractal integration?

Once again, the comparison of different and sometimes opposing approaches can inspire us to find new paths. Let us look at education in the West and in the East. If the Western approach is conceptual and deductive, the Eastern approach is more pragmatic and inductive. Clearly we need to qualify this statement according to the subjects being taught, the different traditions, and also the pupil's age. However, the closer we come to excellence in the West, the more we move towards the conceptual. And thus it is the teacher who explains. And the best teacher is the one who explains best. Similarly, the best pupil is the one who understands best. Excellence lies in deducing.

On the contrary, the greatest Chinese masters (read Fabienne Verdier, for example, in *The Dragon's Brush*[7]) or Japanese ones (read, for example, *Zen in the Art of Archery*[8]) are the ones who know how to repeat the right gesture. They get the student to reflect excellence through the practice of repetition. And the good pupil is one who at times does not seek to understand but lets himself go in the practice of the ritual. Excellence lies in inducing.

These two approaches are, in fact, very much linked to two very different visions of time, linear or cyclic, which we explained in Part 2. Thus in a typically Western linear vision, what matters is the end. And in order to reach it, we must first understand where we are going. The

---

[7] VERDIER Fabienne, *The Dragon's Brush: A Journey to China in Search of a True Master*, Trumpeter, 2006

[8] HERRIGEL Eugen, *Zen in the Art of Archery*, Vintage, 1999

attaining of the goal is deduced by a good understanding of the situation. In a typically Eastern cyclic or circular vision of time, what counts is the form, the process. Thus if we follow the right rituals and protocol, we will attain the goal – even if we did not know it at the start! Good practice induces the best result.

An integral education will help us organize both the stages of repetitive learning and of conceptual understanding. Systems of this type of education which are more inductive, less normative and help students discover their qualities, do exist and have even proved themselves for a good number of years; Sri Aurobindo International Centre of Education, Auroville, the Steiner and Montessori schools, etc.

We could think of going even further with this integration in a more fractal way by finding means to integrate understanding in the repetitive mode of learning, and by knowing how to introduce repetition in the exercise of understanding and deduction. The technological means available to us are surely avenues to explore in our effort to better deepen and spread these integral and fractal educational approaches. For example, video games and MMOG (Massively Multiplayer Online Game) strike me as particularly interesting means of integral and fractal education.

A less linear allocation of spaces and of learning ages

In order to conduct an interesting experiment, Grace Living Center – a nursing home in the town of Jenks, Oklahoma – associated itself with a nursery and a primary school named Jenks School (District of Tulsa). They set up a school with transparent glass walls in the center of the main hall of the nursing home. Every day young students of different ages got reading lessons here. The retired people going past this unusual class very promptly offered their services. A special program of tutor-partner was set up: it paired a student and a resident of the nursing home, the adult listened to the child read aloud and then in his turn read out stories to him. The results? Astounding. These students had much better results in reading tests than other schools. They were even a few years ahead! But there were other even more stunning results. The students didn't just read and listen to the old people, they also discussed with them plenty of other things. The students asked the older ones if IPads were bigger or smaller in their time… Often they had very rich discussions and about the differences of life-style in the different periods.

This apparently helped in the awakening of the student's consciousness. These children not only had better results in reading, but in other subjects too! There were such a large number of parents wanting to put their children in this somewhat special school that they came up with a lottery system to handle the very long waiting list!

But the story does not end there. After a few months of experimenting, the managing board of the old people's home noticed a dramatic decline in the use of sleeping pills and other tranquillizers among the old people participating in this program.

> In 2004, Salman Khan, an American of Indian origin through his mother and Bangladeshi through his father, began helping his niece Nadia to do her math homework. Nadia seems to have been satisfied with her uncle's help and told a lot of her cousins about it. They, in turn, therefore, asked the uncle to help them. Salman felt that it would take him less time if he prepared small clips on YouTube. This was enormously successful with his nephews. They found him much clearer on YouTube than in person! Salman Khan attributes this to the fact that they no longer felt the pressure of the adult over them and could watch the video as many times as they wished and at their convenience. And then, one day he started receiving numerous comments overflowing with gratitude from parents about his videos (which were freely available on YouTube). Dozens, then hundreds, then thousands of thank-you messages from students and parents started pouring in. In 2006, he decided to set up the Khan Academy, a non-profit association that uploads online video lessons. In 2009, he decided that "he could be more useful to society by dedicating himself completely to this activity by resigning from his very well-paid job of a financial analyst on Wall Street" (sic). Bill Gates, in his inimitable style, said of him: "I'd say we have transferred 160 IQ points from the world of finance to the world of education which is effective for the greatest number. It was a great day, the day that his wife allowed him to quit his job!"

Just as I'm writing these lines, there are 4000 lessons online. Volunteers from the whole world are developing new courses in several languages. 150 courses are already available in French, for instance (surely many more by the time you read this book). The website is financed from donations and since 2010, the founder he has refused all forms of advertising.

Salman Khan's idea was to question the traditional model in which students learn all at the same rhythm in a linear fashion, first in the classroom and then with their homework at home. Instead, he offers a model in which students learn at home, when they wish and at their own rhythm. The lessons at school are useful to put into practice and to discuss with the teachers. Several experiments have already been carried out in various schools. The other important point about this new format is that students have been seen to help one another much more spontaneously in a group. The experiment shows the successful setting up of a veritable peer-to-peer teaching structure with students from different parts of the world, of different cultures, in different time-zones, who help one another online!

Through these examples, we can observe the mix of ages in different locations, giving up the linear uniform model for all students, in order to learn at any age: numerous new, more fractal models help in providing a more permanent and lasting education throughout life. An education that is more effective and accessible for a greater number of students. The present day boundaries must be questioned, get rid of the classical, linear model: the nursery school for the very young, the school for the young, the office where one learns less and less, and the nursing home where one learns hardly anything. The geographic boundaries we just saw and also the boundaries of learning-time in our life disappear. We began exploring this in a previous chapter: in a linear life, stages succeed one another: we learn, we use, then we rest. It is time to learn how to learn in a more fractal way. Work during your studies, from a very young age. Fifteen years ago, the USA introduced in the middle and high school syllabus the obligation for students to involve themselves in local social welfare associations for the destitute or for other such causes. Learn to take up studies for a short or long term at any age. Give yourself time to read. Learn to take time off during your work. Take part in technical training programs and personal development workshops.

In a turbulent chaotic world where everything changes and is questioned at every moment, the principal issue of education is: to learn how to learn, to learn how to un-learn, and to learn how to re-learn.

Understanding and developing our organizations

Having looked at the evolution of the human being, of cultures, of relationships between individuals and institutions, of new forms of production and consumption of goods, of new grids of production and consumption of energy, of currencies and of new forms of learning, we shall now focus on how to develop and especially ensure the survival of our organizations in a turbulent and chaotic world. In a general way, when I use the term 'organization', I refer to any type of organization: companies, associations, institutions and other constituted groups which are recognized as such.

The fractal organization

Benoit Mandelbrot says: "If fractals do not perfectly describe nature, then nothing can describe them better." In the preceding chapters we saw that if the vision and the models issued from classical mechanics fitted in well with a world in equilibrium or oscillating close to equilibrium, then a vision and models fashioned on life will help us better to understand and act in a turbulent and chaotic world. In order to adapt, life often chooses forms that we can describe as fractal, especially when optimizing the use of resources and space. Our lungs, therefore, have a fractal form. It is, in fact, natures's best solution for optimizing the intake of air in the largest area possible within the limited volume of the rib cage.

If life has chosen fractal forms in order to ensure its survival, our organizations, our companies can take inspiration from them in order to ensure their survival. Instead of defining here what the organization or the company of the future will be like, we will rather ask

170

ourselves what an organization or company should be to have a future!

We can observe the fractal aspect of organizations at two levels: at the level of the organization or company itself, and at the level of intra-organizations, their ecosystems, the fractal networks of companies or organizations.

In a traditional, mechanistic organization, the boundaries and roles are clearly defined. The boundaries are very clear (or are supposed to be so.). There is the inside of the company and there is the outside. Thus, for example, the boundary with clients lies at the level of sales or marketing teams. The boundary with investors lies at the level of the senior or financial management; the legal boundary lies at the level of the jurists. And so on. What happens is that when we are far from a boundary, we are unaware of what is going on. The production department is unaware of what is happening with clients or with legal aspects. The sales department is unaware of the constraints of investors, etc. This is fine in a world that is changing slowly but it will prove fatal in a chaotic world that is undergoing rapid changes.

With a vision more biological, akin to the living, we can no longer speak of boundaries but rather of membranes. A boundary either lets you pass or it doesn't; it is binary. A membrane's role is to let certain things pass and not others, in certain conditions, at a given time and not at any other. A membrane that delimits a cell also defines it. Without a membrane, a cell cannot exist. And the membrane is also that through which the cell communicates with the rest of the world, especially with regard to its needs for sustenance. It is also through the membrane that the cell unites in order to create a system that is superior to it and of which it will be a part. The membrane, then, both separates *and* unites.

For example, if you are debating whether your personnel should have access to the Internet on their office computer, you are talking about boundaries. If on the contrary, you are discussing about which Internet filters you want to set up, for which websites, or for which type of persons then you are talking about membranes.

Another example of a boundary: the one that exists between working-hours – during which the employee must dedicate one hundred percent of his time to the task assigned by his hierarchy – and leisure-time – during which the hierarchy has no jurisdiction over the activities of its collaborator. We can compare this approach with Google's setting up of a more membrane-type of approach: the rule of twenty percent: twenty percent of the working time is left at the discretion of the collaborator to work on projects that might not have anything to do with the task assigned. It is this membrane approach that has allowed the birth of a number of new Google products, to the delight of the salaried workers who initiated them … and to the great financial advantage of Google!

Thus it might be, for example, a question of setting up processes that allow all the partners of a company to be in direct contact with the 'outside' of the company. It is no longer the static boundaries of an organization or a company that are important, but the dynamic processes that we set up: process of information and process of decision-taking in particular. If, for example, the autocratic decision-making process is perfectly adapted to the army or to pyramidal organizations, if democratic processes are well-adapted to organizations that are already more modern because they are customer-oriented, then we need to turn again to nature and life to go even further and ensure the survival of fractal organizations in a world that has become chaotic by turning to methods issued from Sociocracy.

We shall come back to the regulatory processes and to the decision-making processes a little later in the book.

We can then say, taking inspiration from the fractal images described in the second part and from life, that the principal characteristics of a fractal organization will be:

- **Self-similarity**: each service, each sub-group is organized in a way that is similar to the higher grade or the lower (as in a fractal image).

- **Self-organization**: each sub-group organizes itself according to regulatory processes that enable it to ensure its survival and meet objectives that are compatible with the holistic vision of the organization (like a cell in a living organism). These groups come up and dissolve in a spontaneous way when the objective is reached.

- **Communication**: each sub-group is linked to others sub-groups of the organization due to the strong interdependence made possible by a common vision and by systems of many-sided and widespread communication (as between the cells and organs of a living being). The organism must also be capable of receiving feedback from its external environment, from its ecosystem.

We shall develop these different points in the paragraphs that follow.

Organizations in fractal hives

In a traditional organization, the members are organized in clearly formed teams or in services and for more or less unlimited duration. The whole structure is very clearly hierarchized: there are those who think and decide and there are those who implement. In a more modern organization, we see project-team-based organizations with clearly defined outlines but of limited duration. Those who implement can evidently be invited on certain occasions to participate in the conceptualizing, why even in the decision-making, but it is rare and exceptional. In a fractal type of organization, we go much further and we then see a hive-like functioning emerge – another point of comparison with a living organism. The persons regroup in accordance with tasks that are more or less definite but for a duration that is not determined and may even be sometimes very short. They naturally recede from the hive when they have nothing else to do there and carry on in search of another hive that requires their skills.

It is important to understand that it is not about an organization having only small units or 'islands of production'. A fractal organization will have, on the contrary, units of very diverse sizes as in a fractal image. Some parts of the organization can justifiably be large, for reasons of cost or critical mass, for instance. However, we will find approximately the same types of regulatory processes and processes of self-organization at evry scale.

This process of composition-dissolution will obviously be slower for a sub-group of 2000 persons compared to a team of 20. This is true also for the living organism. The time-scale for a cell, for an organ or for a human being is not the same.

It is important to specify here that in the working of a classical hive, the individuals that compose it (bees, ants) do not have any idea of the overall vision. This is really not fundamental for the good functioning of the whole. On the contrary, in the functioning of what I call a 'fractal' hive, each individual has a vision of the whole at every moment in a dynamic way.

Besides, the physical boundaries of organizations; "I am from such-and-such a site" disappear in favor of more blurred membranes, for instance: "I have the following skills." On the other hand, if one section of the employees or members of the organization can be in the same location, and if others are there for a long duration, others still just come and go occasionally, and there are yet others who work from home or from some other part of the planet.

Similarly, the processes of reflection and decision-making are 'distributed'. Each group, each fractal hive, may be required to take a decision that will impact the totality of the organization. We shall elaborate a little further the systems of fractal governance that should be put in place to ensure a harmonious and efficient functioning of the whole.

In a traditional organization, there is a strategy and a plan of action whose execution is deployed and controlled by the hierarchy. In a fractal hive-like organization, there are processes and regulations that help to bring about a result at the level of the hive. At the level of each hive, these results themselves give rise to an outcome whose contours are not necessarily predictable at the start, at the level of the organization. What is shared by the organization, what is common to all the actors, are processes, regulatory functions and a vision (why we are here together). We shall come back to the importance and the nature of the vision of a fractal organization.

Let us first return to the two indispensable aspects of fractals described in the second part of this book, self-organization and self-similarity, and let us see how these two aspects can help us define our organizations, so they are adapted to survival in a chaotic environment.

Self-organization: how to maintain the survival of a team, an organization, a company, in a chaotic system?

Living organisms, like the construction of a fractal image out of a very simple mathematical formula, have one essential characteristic: self-organization. They possess, in the chaos of their environment, regulatory functions that maintain their existence, such as homeostasis. Homeostasis is the capacity to maintain organisms, or organizations, which are our focus of interest here, in conditions peculiar to life. For example, homeostasis maintains temperature at levels that are acceptable to the life of a cell or of an organism. It eliminates fluctuations that are too great. Homeostasis is thus by definition anti-chaotic. It protects us from turbulence that is too serious or dangerous for the organism. And so, though our body may be exposed to very chaotic conditions of climate and environment, its temperature will not fluctuate much from 37° C – otherwise you would not be able to read this book.

So we speak then of more than control, we speak of regulation or regulatory processes.

It is important to understand the difference between a process control and a process of regulation. Let us go back to the example of the body's temperature. A process control is the loop of negative feedback that we described in the second part of the book. It is thermostat: if it is too hot, the heating gets turned off, if it gets too cold, the heating gets turned on.

A regulatory process can choose, for a limited period and magnitude, of making a positive feedback. For instance, a temperature that is higher than the normal 37°C could be good for your organism and your health. It would enable you to eliminate unwanted microbes and this is a regulatory process which is part of our immune defense system. Here, a process control might be to take recourse to a medicine as soon as the temperature rises, thus forbidding the setting-up of a natural regulatory process of the body.

Obviously too high a temperature can kill the organism and another external regulatory process (your brain or a doctor) could, from a given temperature fixed as too high, decide to prescribe a medicine when your own regulatory process of temperature is weak, which is an unfortunate possibility, if the illness or disease has aggravated.

I am always surprised during my travels to watch my tourist friends rush into taking a medicine against diarrhea as soon as it appears… thus forbidding their organism to set up a regulatory process that tries to get rid of toxins or other harmful elements from their body. There we are clearly in an attempt at control! I am not a doctor but it seems to me that a better external regulatory process, except in rare specific cases, would be to leave the organism to try and eliminate the toxins for a few days… and then see the doctor if that does not work.

Let's take another example: Managers are often faced with a dilemma: 'more control' *or* 'more autonomy' vis-à-vis their collaborators. The advocates of autonomy argue, and quite rightly too, that an excessively hierarchy-based organization that is too centralized, cannot survive in a complex or an unstable environment. The ones in favor of control, argue on the contrary, also quite rightly, that lack of control leads to anarchy – everyone for himself or herself – and the crumbling of the organization. There are several ways of resolving this type of dilemma. Two of the most current ones are: a mix of the two or the polarization towards one of the two extremes. Present-day organizations are often in a kind of alternation, like a swing between two opposites. We can find numerous dilemmas of this kind, for example: should we communicate about our products globally or, on the contrary, develop a more local communication?

There exists, in fact, a third way: finding a solution that rises above the dilemma.

That's exactly what we propose to do here with this analogy of life and cell in biology. A cell is itself constantly faced with the dilemma of 'isolation' or 'communication'. Its survival demands protection and 'isolation' from its surrounding. Without this, it would dissolve and disappear. On the other hand, it must all the time be open to its environment to get information from it or sustenance or even to expel toxins that would prove dangerous to it. It is easy to see how pushing each of the two hypotheses to its extreme leads to the death of the cell. Once more, what life teaches us here is the regulatory process.

Let us take the example of management by objectives in its most ordinary form: 'command and control'. A controller checks if a task has been executed properly in conformity with the plan or objective agreed on. In fact, in a sufficiently stable environment, we will be able to determine in advance an ideal result for an environment that is familiar. But this system is ineffective when the environment becomes unstable and too variable. Organizations will then see that their control mechanisms give way to regulatory functions. A regulator then sets up and checks that the processes selected and agreed upon by the self-organized group, the fractal hive, are properly respected, without often knowing perfectly in advance the anticipated results. It is the respect of these processes that will allow us to obtain the result most adapted to a constantly changing environment. We pass from a mechanistic model of control of results to a fractal and biological model of setting up and verifying processes.

Let us stay with the example of performance control. This is normally controlled at the individual level: individual objectives, verification, individual rewards or sanctions. In a fractal organization, where the individual is significant only at the heart of a self-organized entity, individual performance has no meaning and is not that controllable. The process control of individual is abandoned in favor of a process of objective which is significant only at the level of the group. The regulatory process at the individual level will be a process of accompaniment, a process of personal development, especially at the level of human skills (emotional and relational intelligence, for example). It is then no longer a question of control-reward but a veritable process of coaching available to all at every level of the organization. It is important to point out that this change can happen globally with the same resources. It simply means, for instance, to replace number hours of discussions to fix futile objectives by an equivalent number of hours for coaching.

Process control aim to preserve the existing as it is, and does not allow any major quick changes. The regulatory processes favor, on the contrary, a constant development towards a common vision in the interest of organization members and the organization itself.

Process control is perfectly adapted to ensure the arrival of a train at a certain point (tracks quite rarely move!). Process control is also perfectly adapted to ensure the survival and development of an organization, in a stable environment where changes are rare and of small magnitude. On the other hand, they do not ensure either survival or development in a storm, when environmental changes (new technologies, new entrants into the market, changes in the law, changes in the regulations, fickleness of clients, etc.) are constant and rapid. Regulatory processes are better adapted to ensuring the arrival of a ship safely to a harbor during a storm.

To sum up and compare with Japanese archery (referred to at the beginning of this third part), we can say that regulatory processes:

- Help in the emergence of Beauty: a vision that is shared, inspiration, permanent creativity.

- Encourage Goodness: common culture, links, interdependence of organizational components and of all concerned parties including those outside the organization (for example, authorities, banks, shareholders, etc. in the case of a company).

- Ensure the maintenance of the search for Truth: the reality of financial aspects, a respect for rules and laws.

We shall now focus on how practically to set up the regulatory processes of our organizations.

Regulatory processes in organizations

> At the beginning of a seminar that I was conducting
> for a client, I began by asking each participant to
> introduce themselves. I was really astonished to see
> that though the seminar was happening in French,
> I could not follow twenty percent of what the
> participants were saying and I would have found it
> hard to say even very roughly what each one's
> function was. I asked myself whether I was a
> victim of a flash attack of aphasia. To my great
> relief, I realized that the participants were using a
> vocabulary full of acronyms which did not mean
> much to anyone outside their circle. Everybody is
> not supposed to know that a "SPOC" is not
> something straight out of *Star Trek* but means
> "Single Point of Contact".

In rapidly and constantly changing organizations, it is
essential to check that a certain vocabulary is known by
the entire staff working in an organization.

Here are the first two examples of the regulatory process:

- Check that all the members of the
  organization use a common language.
- Ensure that newcomers in the organization
  become familiar with this common language.

Albert Libchaber, another important contributor to the
theories of chaos, explains that biological systems and
living organisms utilize their non-linearity – the fact that
they are not perfectly regular –, to protect themselves
from noise and external disturbance. So the cardiac
rhythm and the nervous system are capable of preserving
their unique characteristics even in the presence of noise,
something that they would not be able to do were they

perfectly regular. In such a case, the least disturbance could modify their rhythm with significant consequences. By analogy, one could say that an organization that functions in a very rigid way because of its process control will be exposed to the danger of environmental noise, especially when the environment changes very abruptly. On the contrary, the non-linearity of a functioning that is based on more supple and smooth regulatory processes will allow the organization to ensure its existence and growth.

In order to set up regulatory processes, we could create a new post, that of a regulator. Here are a few examples:

- The *ambience setters*: regulators of ambience, they are responsible for creating an atmosphere conducive to work or to exchange that is of a good level.

- The *sociocracy experts:* regulators of governance, they are responsible for communicating the rules of governance or sociocracy and ensuring that they are known and understood by all.

- The *mediators*: regulators of conflict, they help in resolving conflicts by respecting the ethical code of the organization.

- The *experts*: regulators of knowledge, they are responsible for making the best of knowledge available in a given field. They could, for instance, maintain an internal blog, a wiki or a forum on a given subject.

- The *reporters*: regulators of information, they are veritable internal journalists, specialists of story-telling, who go around collecting information (and not just information that comes down from the top of the hierarchy).

- The *official geeks*: technological regulators, they are responsible for the sharing and mastery of the best technologies of information by everyone.

- The *innovators*: regulators of innovation, they are responsible for the sharing of the best techniques of creativity.

- The *godfathers* and *godmothers*: regulators of integration, they are responsible for properly integrating the new members of the organization. This is all the more important as these newcomers are increasingly more diverse.

- The *coaches*: regulators of skills, they ensure that each member of the organization progresses on their own path of growth.

- The *incubators*: The pioneer hunters in the organization, they are on the lookout for those who adopt new approaches, new methods and new tools. The 'early adopters'. They spot them, perhaps assemble them and ensure that they have access to an open space for meetings and exchange, real or virtual. They protect them from the weight and the resistance of the rest of the organization. The incubator knows that new ideas, new approaches that will be validated by the pioneers, will then spread naturally like a virus through the rest of the organization.

- Etc.

At Google, every Friday, the 10,000 persons in Mountain View, California, in addition to the 10,000 others elsewhere are invited to a virtual meeting of an hour with the bosses. And it is 'Google Moderator' who chooses the questions that will be put to them, all this on the basis of a collective vote.

Another example of regulation is creating spaces for exchange to deal with tensions, allowing everyone to express themselves on their anxieties and doubts, and asking questions. It is also complementing the masculine side of the management of the project with a more feminine side that consists in listening and being inclusive. This can obviously be a virtual space.

Elsewhere, at Zappos (leader of Online sale of shoes), the employees, on connecting to their PC session with their password, at once see on their screen an employee of the company chosen randomly. The aim is to enable the employees to know one another, even those who work far away.

> From 1587 to 1983, the Vatican designated a person to argue against the probable canonization of somebody. The former had to find the flaws committed by the latter, flaws that would go totally against the canonization of the person in question. It was a regulatory process that stopped the canonization to sainthood of a person by mistake. It is noteworthy that after John-Paul II discontinued this practice, 500 persons were canonized during his reign as compared to 98 canonized during the reign of all his predecessors in the twentieth century. And so here's another interesting regulatory process: the *devil's advocate*.

The director a very big company told me one day that once a month he met a new recruit chosen randomly (and not selected by his HR department!), and asked him or her in the course of the 30- to 60-minute meeting, his or her 'astonishment report' ever since joining the company. This happened in a very friendly setting and atmosphere, often in the company restaurant and never in the CEO's office. This allows the director to have the fresh vision of a person who already knows the company a little bit from within, but not so much that he or she has lost the outsider's view! He told me that in this way he often gathered very important information which would never be given to him by the executive committee. Here then is an excellent example of a regulatory process!

It is not a question of adding a multitude of new processes to those existing already. On the contrary, it means choosing only a few regulatory processes adapted to the culture, context and concerns of the organization. As shown by Mandelbrot with fractal images, the complexity needed for realizing the vision of the organization will bloom fully in all its beauty from a very simple formula, with very few components but reiterated repeatedly.

Sport as a process of regulation

> I was conducting a workshop one Friday for an IT company in Sophia Antipolis in southern France. The participants insisted I end the seminar on time. I naturally concluded that they had to leave a little earlier for their weekend trip. After packing my things, I got ready to leave the premises by taking the elevator. I was going down from the third story to the first but accidentally I pressed the second story button instead. What a surprise when the doors of the elevator opened on to a large stage. The entire personnel of the company was engrossed in a roller-skating competition! I understood then why it was so important for me to finish my seminar on time: the participants of my seminar did not wish to miss the opening of the fortnightly roller-skating race of the company.

Sport is a regulatory process that is essential in human relationships. Nobody can be forced to play. The choice to do so is free and voluntary. It is through play that we learn, re-learn, to participate in the execution of a common project along with other participants. It is also through play that we learn and re-learn to be ourselves and to offer our uniqueness to the group, the collectivity. It is sport that releases individual creativity. Today, we can do sport among millions as in the Massively Multiplayer Online Game. It is important, then, to introduce in our organizations the possibility and pleasure of playing together. Sport is one of the most important regulatory processes.

Diversity in a fractal organization

Ross Ashby in *Introduction to Cybernetics* shows us that it is only diversity that is capable of responding to the diversity of the environment. In a traditional organization, we look for the norm, for uniformity – we want to see 'just one head'. In a fractal organization, it is diversity that we seek first and foremost. What connects the organization, what ensures its existence, its homeostasis, is no longer the culture of uniformity, but rather a shared vision and a set of common values. A traditional organization puts into place process control by recruiters, head-hunters and by human resource services in order to ensure the compatibility of new recruits. A fractal company to ensure its survival in a chaotic world, would rather go on a hunt for diversity, for fresh new blood. It would, of course, set in place regulatory processes to ensure a smooth and effective integration for the newcomers (cf. above 'godfathers').

What vision for a fractal company or organization?

We have underlined that in a fractal organization, more than in a classical one, vision is an essential element. It is the binder or cement of the organization, the equivalent of a constant inflow of energy necessary for the survival and development of the organization. For those specialists of the chaos theories, the vision of the organization or the company is like the 'strange attractor' of the sciences of chaos. Whatever happens, whatever the uncertainties and the unexpected risks, the organization will continue to move towards this vision like a river which, despite all the climatic circumstances (frost, drought, rains, even the construction of a dam), always adapts instantaneously and inexorably meets the sea, a veritable attractor of the river.

The role of a fractal manager will obviously be, then, to elaborate the unifying and structuring vision and to define the objectives that constitute the attractors of the organization he is called to manage. What objectives will be stable enough as answers to the needs of life and to the ecosystem of the organization or the company?

To continue with this aquatic metaphor, the fractal manager will be both the one who defines the vision, like the sea attracts the river, which will be the attractor of the company. He will also be capable of recognizing and utilizing the currents rising in the whirlpools of his chaotic environment.

The systems of information in a fractal organization

Ilya Prigogine, one of the most eminent contributors to the sense of complexity and chaos, tells us, taking the example of the convections that form in a liquid which is being heated, that matter is blind to equilibrium and begins to 'see' when it becomes turbulent. The comparison is immediate: for a fractal organization to run well in an increasingly chaotic world, its 'agents' (individuals or a group of individuals who are self-organized) must 'see' the totality of the organization. We go from panoptism (only one person has the vision of the whole) to holoptism (everyone sees the whole). The vertical flow of information is replaced by a horizontal flow of information. As in Facebook, you can see where your friends or colleagues are and what they are up to; you can see who does what, how each one performs, who has which skills, etc.

Thus in a fractal type of organization, internal communication within each self-organized group and within other groups or levels of organization becomes fundamental. The systems of information should enable one in particular:

- to share the vision, the reason or purpose, the objective of the organization as a whole.

- to know one's position in relation to one's personal objectives and to other self-organized groups. It means having a system of GPS navigation that shows constantly where we are and where we are heading, and this for all the levels of the organization.

We see then that the priority is for systems that are very supple, very 'user-friendly'. These systems must be capable of constantly re-organizing themselves in relation to the needs and demands of their users. Certain ERPs (Enterprise Resource Planning) today whose aim is the centralization of information for the principal usage of the management are no longer useful. They even weigh down the organization and hinder its agility. Instead, look for systems such as Google Map! Farewell large centralized systems. Long live Facebook clones or Twitter, wikis, blogs, etc. Organization chart, anyway never up-to-date in a turbulent world, are replaced with a mixture of Google Maps and Facebook that allows to identify and locate contacts you need, when you need it.

The fractal manager

Fractal organizations are not 'flat', without hierarchy. As in a human body, all the cells are 'equal' but some have a leading role for other cells to follow, like the brain cells, for instance, that act on other cells of the body. So fractal organizations have in their core what we could call organizing agents. Directors and managers as we know them are going to disappear. The fractal manager resembles very little the manager as defined by Fayol: foresee, organize, command, coordinate, control. He will be replaced by visionaries, regulators, animators and artists. Each person, in keeping with the fractal way, will obviously combine in a lesser or greater degree all the three functions.

In a fractal organization, managers, like fractal images themselves, are 'process driven' guided by the processes and not by the results as they are in a 'result driven' style of management. So, as in the Mandelbrot set, or as in any other fractal image, the fractal manager limits himself to giving simple instructions and allows for the free emergence of very complex but harmonious results. He provides the vision and puts in place regulatory processes.

The fractal manager is aware that he cannot control everything in an increasingly chaotic environment. On the other hand, he learns how to influence. Influencing means taking someone where he did not really wish to go at the beginning, all the while with his consent and respecting his freedom to refuse or change his mind. (Manipulating, on the contrary, is leading him to a place where he did not wish to go without his consent, by cheating and concealing things from him, by threatening or forcing him.)

The fractal manager is a great chef or a painter-artist. He knows how to use the right measure of this or that approach, more or less innovative (he must be therefore familiar with them). He also knows how to use the right measure of diversity in the teams. So, as mentioned above, if diversity is essential during moments when innovation is most important, one must also be able to trim the team's diversity when we seek less innovation and more stability, or when we need to have very fast execution of an occasional well-defined task.

The fractal manager knows how to administer the right dose of 'binder' between all the ingredients and making sure that there is a sufficient degree of communication, connectivity and interdependence between the members of an organization.

He sees clearly where he wants to go but is not so sure about how he wishes to go there. He gets the tools ready as well as the ingredients and the regulatory processes which will enable the great work to emerge and which will ensure the success and survival of the organization.

It is essential to understand that this is not simply about replacing one approach of management with another, newer and more in vogue. This is about questioning the approach of management technics. Instead of replacing outdated versions with a new approach, it means allowing the co-existence, in a fractal manner, of versions which may be old but are more adapted to the culture of the group members, it also means allowing the problem to be solved with an appropriate approach that helps us to ensure the survival of an organization in a chaotic world.

At times, we see the appearance, among regulatory processes, of activities that would be described today as belonging to the old schools, being somewhat 'paternalistic' for instance. But what might appear to be regressive in a modern world might reappear in other forms as regulatory principles that are indispensable for the survival of an organization.

Here are some examples of activities that can be adapted according to the type of organization or enterprise:

-   Financial aid in times of difficulty to the members of the organization and to the salaried
-   A well-equipped internal medical service that goes beyond regulatory requirement.
-   A free legal aid cell
-   An aid-cell for children's education
-   An Assistance cell for the daily needs of the organizational members, like the 'service points' in big companies which offer services like laundry, organic vegetable baskets, clothes mending, etc.

The first question that a fractal manager must ask himself is: Which approach for what type of person? In fact, this flexible approach is one of his fundamental roles. He can then have a certain type of management with a more traditional, more elderly kind of person, and also be a regulatory visionary with younger people. He will then seek to facilitate the spread in a more organic way, through viral contagion, of the fractal approach described in the book to the totality of the organization, as, because he knows that it is only this approach that can ensure the survival and development of his organization in a world that has turned turbulent and chaotic.

The fractal manager, like the true artist, does not possess perfect knowledge of the final task but has a clear vision of what he wishes to achieve. And he masters the processes that will enable him to achieve this vision. He also knows that uncertainty is his friend. He knows that a good manager is unable to control, limit uncertainty, which was the right choice in a world close to balance. Today the manager knows that managing well is relying on uncertainty, surfing the waves of change to achieve the vision, which is the only choice in a turbulent and chaotic world.

The fractal leader knows how to build strong relationships within his fractal hives and with other entities from the ecosystem, so they can adapt and self-organize in a constantly changing world. He knows how to see the order in disorder, extract the organization out of chaos. He can hear the melody hidden by the noise.

Time management and priorities in a turbulent and chaotic world

One day, an old professor was appointed to train a group of about fifteen company directors in 'efficient time-management'.

Standing in front of this very select group, the old professor very slowly looked at them one by one, and then said: "We are going to do an experiment." He brought out from under the table that separated him from the trainees, a large transparent aquarium that he placed gently in front of him. Then he took out about a dozen stones big like tennis-balls and placed them delicately, one by one, inside the aquarium. When it was full to the brim and it was impossible to add any more, he raised his eyes towards the students and asked them: "Is the aquarium full?" All of them answered together: "Yes!"

He waited for a few seconds and replied: "Really?" Then he bent down and brought out a container full of gravel from under the table. Very carefully, he poured this over the stones and lightly shook the aquarium. The gravel pieces slipped in between the stones until the bottom of the aquarium. The old professor raised his eyes once more towards his trainees and asked again: "Now is the aquarium full?"

This time, his bright students caught on and one of them answered: "Probably not."

"Fine," the old professor answered. He bent down once more and brought out from under the table a bucket of sand. He carefully poured the sand into the aquarium. The sand filled up the empty spaces between the big stones and the gravel. He turned to them once again:

"Is the aquarium now full?" This time, the students at once replied in a chorus without the slightest hesitation: "No!"

"Fine," answered the old professor. And as his brilliant famous students had anticipated, he filled the aquarium with a pail of water up to the brim.

He now raised his eyes again and asked his group: "What great truth does this experiment teach us?" The most courageous among them thinking of the theme of this training exclaimed: "This shows that even when we feel our daily schedule is completely filled up, if we truly want to, we can always add more meetings and find more things to do."

"No," replied the old professor, "It isn't that at all. The great truth that this experiment reveals to us is: if we don't put the big stones first, we cannot put the rest!"

There was a deep silence as each one thought about the obviousness of his conclusion. So the old professor continued: "What are the big stones in your professional life and your personal life?"

What is important to remember is precisely the importance of putting the big stones first. If we give importance to trifles (gravel, sand), we will fill up our schedule and our life with trifles and we won't have enough valuable time to dedicate to the important elements.

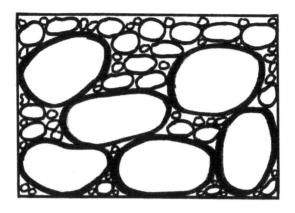

The aquarium of fractal priorities

Does the image of the aquarium filled with big stones, then with gravel and finally sand, make you think of something? A fractal image, obviously!

In a fractal organization, time-management and the choice of priorities becomes even more important than in a classical organization. Time management becomes, in fact, like the cardiac rhythm or the breathing of a living being, an indispensable element for the survival and development of the organism.

The fractal manager always has a precise vision of priorities and he shares it. He knows how to interlink them with less important tasks and preserve the holistic vision (filling the aquarium!), all of this immersed, like the water of the old professor, in the regulatory processes he will have put in place.

Fractal methodology for resolving problems

I would like to conclude this third part by focussing on a question that touches both the members of an organization individually and the organization as a whole. How to resolve a problem in a turbulent environment? How to see through a project successfully in the long-term when everything keeps changing all the time and the world is more and more chaotic?

Let us focus first, by simplifying, on the two ways of resolving problems that are available to us at present: one is conceptual, the other is contextual. The conceptual form dominates Western thinking while the contextual form dominates Eastern thinking (except Japan maybe). These two approaches are also linked to the two very different visions of time we talked about earlier: linear for Westerners, circular and cyclic for Easterners.

In the conceptual approach, first we think, we analyze. First we need to understand. We look for the relevant concept, the working principle, the root causes of a problem. We do not act until we know 'where we are going'. Once we have understood, we have found the root causes of a problem; then we can define our 'strategy', our 'action plan.' It is a linear, analytical process.

Conceptual problem solving is linear

The conceptual resolution of a problem is no doubt the most powerful and certain way for resolving very complex problems within very stable environments. On the other hand, if your environment is not sufficiently stable, it is completely useless.

In the contextual approach, one looks more for the 'significant detail', the detail that will help us in our attempt to resolve a problem. One looks for 'where to stick the rubber patch' or how to go around the problem. One looks for an opportunity and one tries at once. We'll see if it works, and if it doesn't work, we'll try something else. It is a cyclic and reiterated process.

Contextual problem solving is cyclic

The contextual resolution of a problem is indeed ideal for problems that are less complex in very unstable environments. It 'fits in' with their context and even adapts to its rapid changes.

Well, today the challenge is to be able to resolve increasingly complex problems in environments that are also more and more unstable! It is therefore indispensable to put a methodology in place, or rather different methodologies which are both linear *and* cyclic.

Taking the conceptual-linear method and the contextual-cyclic one, seemingly opposite and incompatible, we can evolve new methods where we think and analyze but where, at the same time, we test and experiment. What we might call a more fractal method of sorts!

Complex problem solving is fractal

If there is a domain where we have problems that are very complex and the environment keeps changing permanently, it has to be that of software development. The software developers faced this problem very early on: how to meet the customer's objective when he keeps changing his mind all the time and technology keeps evolving unceasingly?

It isn't surprising at all that it is software development which is most advanced in the resolution of complex problems in an unstable environment. Also the methods that have been put in place there considerably resemble the description I am going to give you about the Agile methodology, in particular.

The Agile methodology implies the involvement of the client and allows for great reactivity to his demands. It is based on a repetitive, incremental and adaptive development cycle.

The Agile methodology advocates, amongst others, four values which will certainly ring a bell about things discussed previously:

- The team: the individuals and their interaction are more important than the tools or the working procedures. It is preferable to have a well-knit team that inter-communicates, composed of developers (maybe of different levels) rather than a team composed of experts/specialists each working alone in their own way. Inter-communication is a fundamental notion.

- The application: operational software programs are more important than exhaustive documentation. They are vital for the application to work. The rest, notably the technical documentation, is a valuable aid but not a goal in itself.

- Collaboration with the clients is more important that contractual negotiation. The client must be involved in the development. We cannot just limit ourselves to the negotiation of a contract before the start of the project, then neglect the demands of the client. The client must collaborate with the team and provide a continuous feedback on the adaptability of the software with his expectations.

- Accepting change is essential. Adapting to change is more important than the follow-up of a plan. The initial plan must be flexible so that it can accommodate the demands of the client throughout the project.

Whatever be your domain, if you are confronted with the necessity of resolving complex problems in an unstable environment, I invite you to study the Agile methodology. This could be a good basis to start putting in place the approaches described in these chapters on the evolution and survival of our organizations in a world become increasingly turbulent and chaotic.

Conclusion

Emergence or breakdown

A very small cause which escapes our notice determines a considerable effect that we cannot fail to see; and then we say that this effect is due to chance.

Henri Poincaré

A bright future: emergence is possible

Rome was the first city to surpass one million inhabitants. It was the first city to reach such a level of complexity (food supplies, water supply, waste-water drainage, waste-disposal, etc.) that it became possible for one million people to live in the same place. After its collapse in 476, the population fell below 100,000 inhabitants.

One had to wait till 1820 before London, during the industrial revolution, became the first city to reach a complexity that enabled it to surpass once again one million inhabitants – that was 1300 years later.

Who can say how much time humanity would take to reconstitute itself if it were to collapse today?

Breakthrough or breakdown? that is the question we face today and that is what makes the era we are living in undoubtedly one of the most fascinating in the history of humanity.

A well-known chaotic phenomenon example of hydrodynamics is the Bénard instability (the scientists speak here of dissipative structure). In this experiment, we heat a liquid from below. When there is a sufficiently large difference of temperature above and below, vortices appear in which billions of particles follow one another. Non-equilibrium creates long-range correlations. As we already pointed out, Ilya Prigogine loved stating that matter in equilibrium is blind, each molecule 'perceiving' only the molecules immediately around it. On the contrary, non-equilibrium leads matter to 'see' the whole and in this way a new coherence emerges from chaos – a beautiful turbulence.

The analogy is easy. When humanity is close to equilibrium and linear, mechanistic laws apply, we only notice those who are close to us – family, tribe or nation in accordance with their level of evolution. When the increase in the number of persons and the volume of interaction does not allow a mechanistic vision to operate, when the 'humanity system' has become chaotic, then the human beings who constitute this system are in a position to see the whole of humanity. Only then can emerge a world consciousness and vision, and even cosmic by incorporating into it nature and the totality of living beings.

Evolution is the fruit of a ceaseless battle between order and disorder, entropy and the emergence of order. From this titanic struggle chaos comes forth out of the delicate balance between the atomic forces and those at the human scale. It is this delicate and improbable balance that is the source of the evolution of life and of consciousness.

That which is at the source of chaos – the increase in number, the increase in exchanges (telephone, internet, travel) – enables one to develop a cosmic and global vision. It is this increase in the volume of interaction and exchange which generates turbulence and chaos, and permits the emergence of a level of complexity needed for living harmoniously among several billion human beings even while we respect our only habitat, this planet earth, our home.

Long live the butterflies!

One evening, the meteorologist Edward Lorenz forgot to switch off his computer where he had programmed a simulation for meteorological forecast. His computer, on its own, calculated the weather forecasts for several days although Lorenz had forgotten to remove the last decimals from his parameters, the thousandth, ten thousandth and the hundred thousandth. When he returned to the computer, Lorenz realized that the final weather portrait was totally different from what he would have obtained if he had removed those famous last decimals (which he had thought to be almost worthless, so very infinitesimal they were in the initial data).

Thus was born what is called 'the butterfly effect.'

He discovered that in meteorological systems, one can never forecast the weather with accuracy, for a variation of some very minor phenomenon, such as the fluttering of butterfly wings, could alter the initial conditions sufficiently to provoke enormous changes after some time. The final result will be totally unpredictable, even if we think we are using the same data as the ones used at another period of which the most important conditions are almost identical. In weather forecasts, a simple infinitesimal action can inevitably provoke totally unforeseen consequences. This is what made him say, "The simple fluttering of a butterfly's wings in Japan can unleash a few weeks later a storm in New York."

Today, a few words on a smartphone can unleash a revolution in some country...

He who has understood that the world is far from equilibrium, that its workings are no longer linear and binary but chaotic and turbulent, understands that one single action, one single project, one single individual transformation can change the world. Thus social transformations are increasingly linked to a few individual actions rather than to mass phenomena. This is because the essential conditions for the emergence of the butterfly effect are more than ever gathered.

If classical mechanics taught us that the same causes produce the same effects, the theories of chaos teach us just the opposite! The same causes do not necessarily produce the same effects! Or more precisely, even the slightest difference in the initial conditions can lead to a completely different result.

All these elements place the power to transform the world in our hands and within our reach, for in such a chaotic situation, the slightest modification can tip everything over. In a linear world, we need to be sufficiently large in number or sufficiently powerful to 'change the world'. In a turbulent chaotic world, a simple little action by an individual can change everything.

Never in the history of humanity has a single human being had so much power. Never in the history of humanity, have YOU had so much power!

Optimistic or pessimistic, it is like being a spectator of a film of which we seem to know the ending, whether happy or unhappy. Today, one must cease to be a passive spectator but an actor in this fast-changing world. I am certain that you will know how to become an actor or an actress in this changing world, a butterfly who will metamorphosize itself and participate at the same time in the metamorphosis of our civilization. And if you see a butterfly around you, a pioneer, help it to flower. Protect it. Make sure that it does not get crushed for it is probably he, or more likely 'she', who will save the world.

So there we are! I am confident that after reading this book, you will no longer see the world as before. Now you will be able to see the ships and understand that factories can work without stock. You will understand the evolution of our world; you will know how to give meaning to something that had none. You will know how to recognize the order that is emerging from the present disorder. You are ready to become the butterfly.

Bibliography

Here is a bibliography. It is not exhaustive on the subject in question but it lists some of the books I have read which have contributed to my thinking and to the elaboration of this book. Some are directly linked to the subject, others less so. This list will either help the curious reader to go deeper into the question or to understand the context in which my ideas and my book came to be.

ANDERSON Chris, 2009, *Free*, Pearson; 2006, *The long tail,* Hyperion book

CARR Nicholas, *Is Google Making Us Stupid?*; 2013, *The big switch*, W. W. Norton & Co

DIAMOND Jared, 1999, *Guns, Steel and Germs,* W. W. Norton & Co.; 2006, *The Third Chimpanzee,* Harper Perennial; 2011, *Collapse,* Penguin Books

GLADWELL Malcom, 2001, *The Tipping Point,* Little, Brown and Company, 2006, *Blink,* Penguin, 2009, *Outliers*, Back Bay Books; 2010, *What the dog saw*, Back Bay Books

GLEICK James, 2008, *The Theory of Chaos*, Penguin Books

HEATH Chip & HEATH Dan, 2007, *Made to Stick*, Random House; 2010, *Switch*, Crown Business; 2013, *Decisive*, Crown Business

HOVERSTADT Patrick, 2008, *The fractal Organization*, Wiley

KAHN Salman, 2012, *The one world school house*, Twelve

KAWASAKI Guy, 2011, *Enchantment, The art of changing hearts, minds and actions*, Penguin

KLEIN Naomi, 2008, *The Shock Doctrine*, Picador

LAZLO Ervin, 2007, *Science and the Akashic field*, Inner Traditions

MAALOUF Amin, 2003, *In the Name of Identity*, Penguin Books

MANDELBROT Benoît, 2006, *The Misbehavior of Markets*, Basic books,

MARION Bruno, 2009, *Prospective d'un monde en mutation*, L'Harmattan; 2008, *Réussir avec les Asiatiques*, Eyrolles

McINTOSH Steve, 2007, *Integral consciousness*, Paragon House

MORIN Edgar, 2008, *On complexity*, Hampton Press; 1999, *Homeland earth*, Hampton Press

NOUBEL Jean-François, 2004, *Collective Intelligence, The invisible revolution*, noubel.com

NOWAK Martin, 2011, *Supercooperators*, Canongate Books

PRIGOGINE Ilya, 1997, *The end of Certainty*, Free Press; 1984, *Order out of Chaos*, Bantam; 2003, *Is Future Given?* World Scientific Pub Co Inc, 1981, *From Being to Becoming*, W H Freeman & Co

REICH Robert B., 1992, *The work of nations*, Vintage

RIFKIN Jeremy, 2014, *The Zero Marginal Cost Society*, Palgrave Macmillan; 2013, *The third Industrial Revolution*, Palgrave Macmillan; 2009, *The Empathic Civilization*, Tarcher; 2005, *The European Dream*, Tarcher; 2001, *The Age of Access*, Tarcher; 1996, *The end of work*, Tarcher;

RUELLE David, 1993, *Chance and Chaos*, Princeton University Press
TALEB Nassim, 2014, *Antifragile*, Random House; 2010, *The Black Swan*, Random House; 2005, *Fooled by Randomness*, Random House
TAPSCOTT Dan, 2008, *Grown Up Digital*, McGraw-Hill; 2007, *Wikinomics*, Pearson
TAYLOR Jill Bolte, 2009, *My Stroke of Insight*, Plume
TOFFLER Alvin, 1991, *Powershift*, Bantam; 1984, *Future Shock*, Bantam; 1984, *The Third Wave*, Bantam
WARNECK H. J., 1993, *The fractal Company*, Springer-Verlag
WILBER Ken, 2007, *Integral Spirituality*, Shambhala; 2007, *Integral Vision,* Shambhala; 2001, *Grace and Grit*, Shambhala; 2001, *A Theory of Everything*, Shambhala ; 2001, *Sex, ecology and spirituality*, Shambhala ; 2001, *A History of Everything*, Shambhala; 2000, *One Taste*, Shambhala; 2000, *Integral Psychology*, Shambhala

For more and updates please visit:

www.brunomarion.com

66730374R00138

Made in the USA
Charleston, SC
29 January 2017